HARRY THE POLIS
UP TAE MY NECK IN PAPERWORK!

• • •

HARRY MORRIS

BLACK & WHITE PUBLISHING

First published 2009
by Black & White Publishing Ltd
29 Ocean Drive, Edinburgh, EH6 6JL

1 3 5 7 9 10 8 6 4 2   09 10 11 12 13

ISBN 978 1 84502 262 4

Typeset by RefineCatch Ltd, Bungay, Suffolk

Printed by CPI Cox & Wyman, Reading

• • •

This book is dedicated to
ME!
I've never had anything dedicated to me
before, so this dedication is a first

This book is therefore officially dedicated to:

Harry Morris
aka
Harry The Polis

• • •

JUST A COP

...

The funeral line was long, with an awful lot of cars.
Punters appeared from offices, restaurants and bars.
A worker on a building site let his hammer drop.
Someone asked, 'What's this all about?'
The reply was, 'Just a cop!'
Some sniggered at the passing cars, others shed a tear.
One said, 'This is stupid, all these dumb polis here!'
'How come they're not out fighting crime?
Or in a coffee shop?
Seems like an awful lot of bother, for someone who's
just a cop!'
They blocked off intersections and traffic had to wait.
A driver voiced his disapproval that this would keep him late.
'This is totally ridiculous, signalling us all stop! If nothing it's
a waste of time for someone who's
just a cop!'
Into the cemetery now, the funeral procession arrived.
A lone piper played a lament, as friends and family cried.
A graveyard worker shook his head. 'A bit over the top!
Lots of words all totally wasted on someone who's
just a cop!'
Yes, 'just a cop' to most folk, who did his duty every day.
Trying his best to protect us, till his life was taken away.
So when he got to heaven, St Peter put him at the top.
And when an angel asked, 'Who was that?'
he replied, 'Who him?
He's just a cop!'

Anon.

Adapted and arranged by Harry Morris

Contents

• • •

Introduction   xiii

PART ONE   1
Lovely Boy!   1
The Affair   5
Not a Neck Chain   6
The Winner   6
Wrong Answer!   7
Dyslexic Robbers   8
Finding a Cure!   9
Sports Wear   10
The Interview   11
The Sex Therapist   13
Walking the Dog   14
Breaking News   14
Spiritual Guidance   15
Love on the Road   17
Lardy Spice   18
Rank has its Privileges   19
Ryanair Flight 7842   20
Nearly Right, Ma'am!   26
Smart Answer   27
Harry's Help Page   28
The Reply   29

PART TWO   30
Tell him Anything!   30
Polis Nicknames   32

Written in Advance   33
Taking the Piss!   34
Sweaty Betty   35
Bath Night   36
Morris's Text News   37
The Dentist   39
Ring Back   40
Smart Answer   41
Erotic Nights   42
Beg Your Pardon   44
Keep the Tip!   45
Change of Job   47
Begging Your Pardon?   48
Early Retirement Bonus   49
Friendship Between Police   50
Mistaken Identity   51
Good Manners   52
Alternative Weekend   53

PART THREE   55
New Breed   55
Case Solved   56
The Robbery   57
Diarrhoea!   58
Pray for Me!   59
Daddy's on the Phone   60
Horth Withperer   62
Cage Rage   63
Check In   64
Russian Mafia   65

Retired Cops' Reunion   69
No-Frills Meals   70
The Ultimate Test   71
You Decide!   73
Career Change   75
Big Burd   75
Rope a Dope   76
Where's the Burd?   78
The Traffic Jam   80
Debt to Society   82

PART FOUR   85
Fancy Dress Party   85
What Birthday?   87
Heed Your Speed!   88
Confession Time   89
Sweet Revenge   90
The Note   91
The Dog   93
Ann Summers' Condiments   94
Old Age is Fun   95
The Twenty Pound Note   97
The Adventures of Harry the Polis   99
Polis Don't Lie!   100
Play Around   101
Private Health   102
D. I. Y. TVs   104
Haemorrhoid Man   106
The Village Bobby   108
Fact or Fiction?   110

The Facecloth 113
I Left it There! 116

PART FIVE 118
The Care Worker 118
Thirty Days 120
Mutual Advice 121
Picking up the Pieces 122
Deathbed Confession 124
The Man who would be King! 126
Deep Shit 127
Medicine Man 128
Glesca, God's Country 129
Fire in the Hole 131
Itchy Powder 132
Get the Point 135
Last Request 136
Spice of Life 137
Old Aged Polis 138
All About Ivy 139
Drunk Aye, Daft Naw! 142
Serenity or Senility? 143
The Court Case 144
Fitness Club 145
Whyte & Mackay Health Drink 146

PART SIX 148
Wee Jock is Back! 148
The Examination 152

Public Complaints   153
Public Complaint   154
The Hoover Man   155
The Glesca Ned   156
The Credit Crunch   158
Bath Night   160
The Fur Coat   162
Beam Me Up!   164
Taxi Fare   166
Missing, Presumed Pished!   167
Good Spirit   170
The Original PC   172
Viagra!   173
Marriage   174
Whisky Fruit Pies   175
It's How You Say It!   178
Fly Guy!   180
Pick 'N' Mix Affairs   182
Dead Funny. Not!   183

PART SEVEN   186
Advent Calendars   186
We Know What He Meant   187
Quick Wit!   187
Horse Talk   189
What's in a Name?   191
American Dragnet Stories   193
Gaetano   195
You Can Be A Polis . . .   211

Harry Says. . . 'Share With Me!'   213
Thank You   215
Acknowledgements   216
Contact Details   216

Introduction

• • •

I'm constantly asked the same questions by friends, acquaintances and ex-colleagues, when I perform my Stand-Up Storytelling, or when I'm occasionally invited along to a book festival, Q &A or Crime Night.

'Don't you miss the police force, Harry? The harmony, the guys on the shift, the excitement you feel in your gut when involved in a good 'bust', culminating with the bad guys getting charged and locked up in a cell?'

My answer is always the same. That part of my life has gone and you have to move on to the next chapter in your life.

Fortunately for me, I've never missed a day, a night, a shift or a court appearance since moving on . . . Why?

Because I write about the funny things, the good times and the many characters whose paths crossed mine and left their indelible mark on me forever.

Some I worked with and some whom I dealt with in my capacity as a police officer doing my job; some are no longer with us, but their stories are and will continue to be told, and along with the humour will last forever.

Therefore, enclosed is another collection of stories, jokes, anecdotes and tales (and lies) about life, which are not to be taken seriously, but are intended to entertain you, the reader, and bring a smile to your face.

'Harry the Polis' is designed to make you laugh and relate a story, joke or anecdote to someone who needs some cheering up. Let's face it, we all know somebody!

Laughter: the best medicine to take!

And best of all, you can never overdose on it either.

Harry

Lovely Boy!

...

I thought I would start by taking you back to the days before I joined the City of Glasgow Police Force.

I had left school prior to my fifteenth birthday, and followed my older brother Allan into the butcher trade.

As luck would have it, I was sent to work in the same shop as my brother, who just happened to be the second hand, or under manager of the shop.

After a couple of years, although still young, I had qualified in all aspects of my trade, and was promoted and transferred to another shop, to carry out the duties of the second hand.

Things were going well for me, up until the painters arrived to brighten up the shop with a fresh 'lick' of paint.

This job was carried out by two painters, employed by the company, to travel around from branch to branch, maintaining the interior and exterior appearance of the shops.

Of the two painters employed, one was Fred, a six feet plus, well-built ex-Royal Marine Commando, dressed in his army combats and boots, like GI Joe.

The second was Cyril.

The total opposite in looks and build to Fred, but he was a Don Estelle look-a-like, from *It Ain't Half Hot Mum*, in that he was small, fat, balding and wearing the old-school NHS spectacles, minus the regulation piece of sticking plaster over one lens.

Cyril also had this annoying habit of either whistling in a high-pitched key, like the bird impersonator Percy Edwards, or singing one song after another – songs like

'Why Do You Whisper Green Grass?' All bloody day long, to the annoyance of myself.

I say myself, because the women customers who entered the shop absolutely loved this wee oddity and his singing voice, and if there was a queue waiting to be served, he would actually take requests and perform for them, with paint brush in hand, held in front of his face like a microphone, while hanging on halfway up a ladder.

'Oh, you're marvellous, you should be on that *Opportunity Knocks*!' Women would tell him, boosting his ego.

Now, for our younger readers, *Opportunity Knocks* was the 1960s equivalent of *The X Factor*, and the host Hughie Green was like Simon Cowell, without the high-waisted trousers.

On this particular day, Cyril was serenading the waiting customers with his musical rendition of the old Gracie Fields lyrical classic, 'Sally', along with various other oldies.

While he was doing this, his partner in paint got in on the act, by acting like Windsor Davies, the sergeant major and master of ceremony, who introduced them all to some corny, old-fashioned jokes, in between little 'Don' actually using the brush to spread some paint on the walls.

All the while, Fred, dressed in his ex-army gear like Barbie's Ken, noted the latest song request and announced it thus:

'The next song is for Isabel Kane, third in the queue, and she would also like to wish her husband Jackie a speedy recovery!' Then he added, 'Apparently, he burnt his face while dooking for chips! But not to worry, he's now reciting poetry in the "Burns" unit of the Royal Infirmary!' Boom! Boom!

And while he was spouting all this mince, little Don Estelle would be singing about everything he saw or heard, things like, 'Right Said Fred, (Cup of Tea).'

This had been the practice for the entire week of their presence at the shop, and I was sick to the teeth of both of them.

Suddenly, without warning, the customers within the shop burst into a crescendo of applause, as little Don finished his latest lyrical selection from his painters' party song sheet.

This also coincided with me losing my concentration for a split second, whilst boning a shoulder of beef, and allowing my boning knife to slip, whereby I subsequently stabbed myself in the groin.

This was the final straw for me, having endured listening to this annoying little twat squawking, albeit melodically, all week and GI Joe spouting out his rank rotten jokes. I'd had enough.

With the boning knife still sticking out of my leg and the resultant blood beginning to saturate my denim jeans, I walked over to his ladder and grabbed hold of it with both hands.

'Okay, lovely boy! The party's over for you,' I announced.

Little Don looked down at me, and as his facial expression quickly changed to one of complete horror, he screamed at the top of his voice, 'Help! I Need Somebody. Help!'

This brought a smile to my face, and I took great pleasure in shaking the ladder vigorously from side to side, with him squealing tunefully while frantically clinging on to the top rung.

Suffice to say, it took my mind off the fact that I had a bloody big knife sticking in my groin having just stabbed myself, but here I was, for the first time that week, really enjoying hearing this annoying little twat's voice, as he screamed uncontrollably, 'Stop! In The Name Of Love! Before You Break My Heart!'

I can assure you, it wasn't his heart I wanted to break!

I did stop – not through choice, but due to the fact that his six-feet-three Marine Commando and minder had his arm around my neck and was physically lifting me off the floor, while blocking off my only airways and depriving me of the oxygen that I required in order to breathe.

Using sign language, and digging my tackety boot heal into his unprotected testicles, I managed to convince him to release his grip and let me go, aided and abetted by other staff and customers within the shop.

Due to the seriousness of my knife wound, I was taken by ambulance to the local hospital and treated.

During my time of incapacity away from the shop, recovering from my injury, Don and Windsor had finished off the painting much earlier than had been anticipated, and had moved on to the next one on their list, via the auditions for *Opportunity Knocks*.

As a result of my serious injury, coupled with GI Joe's attempts to choke me, I left the butchering trade and joined the police. Definitely much safer and less chance of getting injured.

However, twenty-nine years later, having sustained more than my fair share of serious and lasting injuries during my police service, as Cher would say, 'If I Could Turn Back Time'!

The Affair

• • •

A police superintendent was having an affair with his office secretary.

One day, they both went to her house, where they proceeded to make love all afternoon. Totally exhausted, they both fell asleep and didn't waken up until seven o'clock that evening.

The superintendent got up out of bed and quickly got dressed. Whilst doing so, he told his lover to take his black uniform shoes outside and rub them on the grass and dirt.

He then put his shoes on, jumped into his car and drove home.

As he entered the front door of his house, his wife demanded to know, 'Where the hell have you been?'

He looked straight into her eyes and replied, 'I can't tell a lie. I've been having an affair with my office secretary. In fact, I've been making love to her all afternoon!'

She stared into his eyes for a moment, then looked down at his shoes and said, 'You big lying bastard, you've been playing golf again!'

Not a Neck Chain

· · ·

During the 1970s the government introduced a Youth Training Scheme for young people, better known as YTS.

The police had to be seen to be supporting this new idea for giving young people experience and played their part in the scheme.

As a result, they employed several young people in the area to work within the police stations.

Such was the case with a young girl who was employed by the CID to do some simple filing of case reports.

Unfortunately, ABC wasn't exactly a strong point with her, but worse was to follow with her filing skills.

The classic of the day was when she filed a Silver Cross Pram under the heading 'Jewellery'!

The Winner

· · ·

A policewoman arrived home one night, screeching her car to a sudden halt in the driveway. Slamming the car door shut, she ran to the house, burst through the front door and shouted at the top of her lungs, 'Honey! Quick as you can, pack your bags. I've just won the lottery!'

Her husband squealed with excitement, 'The lottery? Oh my God! What should I pack, honey, beach stuff, or winter ski stuff?'

To which she replied, 'I don't really give a shit, honey. Just hurry up and get the hell out my house!'

Wrong Answer!

· · ·

An ex-colleague was sitting up in bed one night, totally engrossed, reading the latest Harry the Polis book (*Ah Cannae Tell a Lie!*), when his concentration was interrupted by his wife who posed the following question:

'Tell me this, John, what would you do if I died? Would you consider getting married again?'

'I don't think so!' he replied before nodding his head and adding, 'No. Definitely not!'

'Why not? Don't you like being married?' she asked.

'Of course I like being married,' he responded.

'Then why wouldn't you re-marry?'

He thought for a moment before responding, 'Okay! Okay! I'd get married again. Happy now?'

His wife was slightly hurt by this response. Her facial expression dropped and she said, 'So, you're now saying you *would* get married again?'

At that, he made an audible groan and turned his attention back to his book.

'Would you set up home in our house?' she continued.

'Sure! Why not? It's a great house,' he promptly replied.

'So you would sleep with her in our marital bed?'

'Well, where else would we sleep?' he asked her.

'Would you let her drive my wee car?'

'Probably! It's almost new,' he responded.

'Would you take my pictures down off the wall and replace them with hers?' she asked him.

'I suppose that would seem like the right thing to do,' he replied.

'Would you give her all my jewellery to wear?'

'Who knows what I would do, but I'm quite sure she'd prefer her own,' he said.

'Would you let her get involved in all your hobbies and take her out golfing with you?'

'Of course I would! They're always good times together,' he responded.

'And would you let her use my new set of golf clubs?' she asked.

To which he immediately blurted out, 'Don't be silly, she's left handed!'

There was a moment of silence before he mumbled under his breath, 'Oh shit!'

Dyslexic Robbers

. . .

Two dyslexic robbers run into a bank and shout, 'Air in the hands, mother stickers – this is a fuck up!'

'YES WAS IT OH!'

(Anagram for those readers who are not dyslexic.)

Finding a Cure

· · ·

I received a call one day to attend at the house of an elderly couple of sisters, one of whom was the local church organist. She was in her eighties and had never ever married.

As a regular churchgoer, she was admired for her sweetness and kindness to everyone in the congregation.

During my visit that afternoon she showed me into her quaint little sitting room and invited me to have a seat in front of the fire while she prepared tea.

As I sat there quietly facing her old Hammond organ, my attention was drawn to a cut-glass bowl sitting on top of it.

The bowl was filled with water and, surprisingly, floating on top of the water, of all things, was a condom!

When she returned to the room with tea and scones, we began to chat.

I tried to stifle my curiosity about the bowl of water and its strange floater, but my curiosity soon got the better of me and I couldn't resist it any longer, so I plucked up the courage and asked her outright.

'Excuse me, ma'am, I hope you don't mind me asking this, but I wonder if you can tell me the significance of this?' I said, pointing to the bowl.

'Oh, yes,' she replied. 'Isn't it just wonderful? I was walking through the park a few months ago when I came across this little package lying on the ground.

'I picked it up and read the directions on the front, which said to place it on the top of the organ and keep it wet.

'It also stated that it would prevent the spread of disease.

'Do you know, ever since I brought it home and did that, I haven't had as much as a cold, never mind the flu, all winter . . . Quite amazing, don't you think?'

Sports Wear
· · ·

Several years ago a number of Strathclyde Police officers were assigned to go to Holland with regards to providing the security in the Lockerbie bomb terrorist trial. All personnel were instructed to take something with them in order to help pass the time and prevent boredom. Some took tennis and badminton racquets, playing cards, swimming costumes, footballs and running shoes, and so on.

However, one officer turned up and appeared to have nothing from the list in his possession. When asked by the duty inspector what he had brought with him to alleviate the boredom, he produced a packet of tampons.

'What are you going to do with them?' asked the inspector.

To which he replied, 'Well it says on the side of the packet that if you wear one of these tampons, you can go jogging, play tennis, go swimming, play card games, dance . . .'

The Interview

• • •

Four police officers of various ranks were being interviewed for a special job. The interviewer asked them all in turn the following question: 'What is the fastest thing you know of?'

The Acting Chief Inspector replied, 'A thought. It pops into your head and there is no advance warning that it's on the way, but it's just there. So, in answer to your question, I would have to say, a thought is the fastest thing I know of.'

'That's very good,' replied the interviewer, then turning to the second applicant – the Inspector –he said, 'And now you, sir.'

The Inspector thought for a moment. 'Hmmm, let me see . . . I would have to say the blink of an eye! It comes and goes and you don't know it ever happened. Therefore, my answer to you, sir, is a blink!'

'Excellent!' said the interviewer. 'The blink of an eye. That's a very popular cliché for speed.' He then turned to the recently accelerated-promoted young sergeant, who was busy contemplating his response to the question.

'Well, over at my parents' home, you step out of the house, and on the back wall there is a light switch. When you flick that switch, a light, over on the opposite side of the yard, next to the horse stables, comes on in an instant, so I would submit to you that turning on a light is, in my opinion, easily the fastest thing I can think of.'

Again, the interviewer was very impressed with the answer and thought he had found his man within this trio.

'I have to admit that it's very hard to think of something faster than the speed of light,' he said, before turning to the final applicant, who just happened to be an elderly Glaswegian sergeant, to pose the same question.

'Well, I've got to admit that after listening to the three previous answers given by my colleagues, it's fairly obvious to me that the fastest thing I can think of is diarrhoea!' he said confidently.

'What?' said the interviewer, totally bemused by the sergeant's response. 'Can you explain to me your answer?'

'Oh, I can explain it alright,' he replied. 'You see, the other night there I was out with the guys on my shift and had lamb vindaloo, followed by several pints of Guinness. Next morning when I awoke for the early shift, I wasn't feeling too good, and had to make a beeline for the bathroom. But before I could think, blink, or turn on any light, I had shat all over my pants!'

Guess what? He got the job!

The Sex Therapist

. . .

A retired cop and his long-term mistress, both in their seventies, walked into a sex therapist's office. The doctor asked, 'What can I do for you?'

The retired cop said, 'Will you watch us while we have sexual intercourse?'

The doctor raised both eyebrows, but he was so amazed that such an elderly couple were asking for his sexual advice, that he agreed to their request.

When the couple finished, the doctor said, 'There is absolutely nothing wrong with the way you are having sexual intercourse.'

He thanked them for coming in, wished them good luck, and promptly charged them £40 for his services.

A week later the couple returned and asked the sex therapist to again watch them, while they indulged in sexual intercourse.

The sex therapist was a bit puzzled, but reluctantly he agreed.

This occurred for several weeks in a row, with the elderly couple making appointment after appointment to have sexual intercourse in his presence, and with no apparent problem diagnosed, paying the doctor for his services before leaving.

Finally, after three months of this repeated routine, the doctor said, 'I'm sorry, but I feel professionally obliged to ask you . . . Just what exactly are you trying to find out?'

The old cop looked at him with a puzzled expression on his face and said, 'We're not trying to find out anything. She's married, so we can't go to her house and have sex. I'm also married, so we can't do it in my house. The Holiday Inn charges £70 for a double room and the Hilton charges £120. So, if we can do it here in your office for £40, I have the added bonus of being able to claim it all back from my BUPA Medical Care.'

Walking the Dog
• • •
Which reminds me of the Dog Branch policeman who was walking his dog through the woods near to his house late one night and accidentally stepped on a man's bare bum.

Suddenly a girl's voice called out, 'Thanks pal!'

Breaking News
• • •
By the end of this year, it has been rumoured that the present government are to give serious consideration into deporting all mentally ill people.

My eyes filled up on hearing this and I became really upset when I thought about you, my loyal reader.

So run like hell, my crazy friend, and don't stop!

Spiritual Guidance

· · ·

One Sunday morning a church parishioner, having just attended the six o'clock mass, surrendered himself to the first police officer he saw on the street, P.C. Ambrose, and openly confessed to the brutal murder of his wife the previous evening.

Due to there being no transport available to attend his location, P.C. Ambrose decided personally to walk the suspect male down the High Street to the divisional headquarters situated in Turnbull Street, a distance of about half a mile, and all carried out whilst securely hand-cuffed to his wrist.

While making his way along the road with his suspect, he met up with Father Lynch, a retired Irish priest residing in the retirement home, who was returning from a housewarming party in the London Road area. The priest was nicknamed Benny by his friends amongst his old congregation, due to being regarded as a very good amateur boxer in his younger days.

After a brief conversation, P.C. Ambrose made him aware of the confession, as told to him by the suspect.

On hearing this information, Father Lynch was totally shocked, having been familiar with the family, but pleaded that the suspect be allowed to confess his sins in the proper way, and as such, he immediately arranged there and then to hear his horrific confession in the High Street.

However, in order for this to be carried out properly, Father Lynch requested that P.C. Ambrose release the suspect from his custody, into his.

P.C. Ambrose reluctantly agreed to the priest's outrageous request by removing the suspect from his cuffs.

Father Lynch put his hand gently on the suspect's shoulder, pulled him towards him and immediately proceeded to punch the living daylights out of him in the middle of the street, displaying all his experienced boxing skills.

A stunned P.C. Ambrose could only stand and watch as Father 'Benny' Lynch landed blow after blow on the suspect's head and body, which he referred to as religious, summary justice.

Fortunately, by sheer coincidence, a police van appeared in the street, and on seeing the disturbance, coupled with P.C. Ambrose waving his arms about frantically to attract them, they pulled over and stopped.

With the assistance of the van crew, P.C. Ambrose was able to restrain Benny and re-arrest his badly beaten suspect.

Father Lynch then accompanied the police officers to the murder scene, where he gave the last rites to the murdered victim.

Lo and behold, the now accused husband refused to make any complaint against Father Lynch.

The bruised and battered accused was charged with the murder of his wife and subsequently pleaded guilty, receiving a custodial life sentence.

As for Father 'Benny' Lynch, he attended the Royal Infirmary where he was diagnosed with badly bruised knuckles and a staved thumb!

Father Benny's totally outrageous actions on that morning gave a whole new insight into making a confession and being handed a religious penance to carry out.

Love on the Road

. . .

I had occasion to attend a road accident on the Glasgow M8 motorway and on my arrival, there were two cars parked on the hard shoulder. One of the parked cars had collided with the nearside barrier.

As I got out of my patrol car to approach them, I heard a groaning noise coming from the other side of one of the cars.

Thinking that the driver was lying injured, I walked around the other side of the car to discover a man and woman engaged in sexual intercourse on the red tarmac of the roadway.

'Here, you two!' I called out. 'What's going on there?' (As if I didn't know!)

They both immediately scrambled to their feet, arranging their disheveled clothing as they did.

'We're very sorry, Officer,' replied the rather embarrassed woman. 'But being a trained nurse, when I saw the road accident, I stopped to give assistance and dragged this man out of his damaged car, and I immediately began to administer mouth to mouth resuscitation and . . . well, one thing led to another!'

Lardy Spice

...

'Lardy Spice' was the nickname of a very large police-woman I had the good fortune to work with. She appeared at the police social club one evening, wearing a bright yellow sleeveless sun dress and resembling a very humongous 'Tweety Pie', who looked like she had just eaten Sylvester the Cat!

As she walked into the centre of the lounge, she raised her right arm, revealing an overgrown hairy armpit, then, wetting her finger, she pointed to all the police officers sitting at the bar and asked, 'What gentleman here would like to buy a lady a drink?'

The entire police club went silent as the patrons turned away to ignore her, but down at the end of the bar, propping it up, an owl-eyed Willie McDermott slammed his hand down on the counter and bellowed out loudly, 'Give the ballerina a pint!'

Jimmy the club master poured the drink and Lardy gulped it down, faster than you can say, 'I taut I taw a puddy tat.'

Moments later, she turned to the patrons seated in the lounge and again pointed at them, revealing the same hairy armpit, and asked, 'What gentleman here would like to buy a lady a drink?'

Again, the owl-eyed Willie McDermott slapped his money down on the bar and said, 'Give the ballerina another pint!'

Jimmy the club master approached the slightly pissed Willie and asked, 'Tell me this, Willie, it's entirely your business if you want to buy the lassie a drink, but why do you keep referring to her as a ballerina?'

To which Willie replied with a straight face, 'Because any woman who can lift her leg that high, has got to be a ballerina!'

Rank has its Privileges

• • •

A married police inspector went off to Perth for a wild weekend with a young policewoman on his shift.

Afterwards, on the way home, he couldn't resist asking her:

'Will you ever be able to forget such a wonderful weekend?'

To which she replied, 'Depends on how much it's worth, sir!'

Ryanair Flight 7842

· · ·

I was trying to book a flight to Spain online, but as I've already told you before, when it comes to computers, my nickname is PC Illiterate, so I'm getting nowhere fast.

I'm even cursing at the cursor. Well why not? Is that not why they called it so?

Anyways, I decide, I'll phone their customer service office, it's £1 per minute, but it'll only take a minute to book it, especially with them doing it all for me, or so I thought.

No chance. The lassie on the other end of the phone answered, 'Hello, Ryanair Customer Service, can I help you?'

So I explained that I wanted to book a flight to Spain. Right away, the wee bitch wound me up.

'How many people are flying with you?' she asked.

'How many people?' I thought. 'How the hell would I know that, hen, it's your bloody aeroplane not mine!'

Not exactly the answer she was looking for, and as a result, she told me to book it online and promptly hung up the phone.

As it was, I ended up down at the library and the girl in there booked my flight for me: Ryanair Flight 7842 to Murcia, Spain.

A week later, I was in Glasgow Prestwick Airport, boarding the plane prior to take off.

As I entered the plane, there was a hold-up in the aisles, and the air hostess just inside the doorway called out, 'Come on, people, we're not picking furniture here, so if you see an empty seat, get your bum on it!'

No wonder they call it the 'no-frills' airline. You have to be able to fight like Mike Tyson to get a bloody seat in the first place – and let me tell you this, on a plane full of Glesca punters, even 'Iron Mike' would be hard pushed to get his arse on one!

However, as luck would have it, I managed to secure a seat at the front right away.

Moments later, an air hostess came up to me and asked me to move, as the seat I was in was already taken.

'Don't think so, hen! You can't reserve a seat on here, it's a case of first come, first served as they say!'

She then became quite aggressive and indignant towards me and threatened me with the usual. 'If you don't move yer backside aff that seat, we won't be taking off and you can explain to this lot of sun worshippers the reason why!'

'Is that right? You're telling me the pilot will not take off, just because I won't move my seat for some late bugger?'

'Naw, ya bam! I'm telling you the pilot can't take off until you get aff his bloody seat!' she announced.

I looked around at all the dials and bright lights and said, 'Well ye only needed tae ask me, hen. I'm not exactly a mind reader!'

Reluctantly, and slightly embarrassed, I moved.

I had only just taken my next seat on the Ryanair flight to Murcia, Spain, when it took off almost immediately, racing down the runway at breakneck speed – that's very fast!

After a few moments, we were up in the sky and the plane had just reached its cruising altitude, when the captain made an announcement to all the passengers on board.

'Ladies and gentlemen, this is your captain speaking. I would just like to welcome you all aboard Ryanair Flight 7842, non-stop from Glasgow Prestwick to sunny Murcia, Spain. The weather for today is looking good, so we should have a very smooth, uneventful flight. With that said, I would now ask you all to sit back in your seats, those that have one, relax and enjoy the— Aarrgghhh! Holy Mother of God!'

This unusual announcement was quickly followed by complete and total silence from the flight deck.

What a sight to behold, as a plane load of Glesca punters bound for the four 'S's (Sun, Sea, Shagging and Sangria) were promptly sobered up.

I myself had just squandered almost £50 in the airport departure lounge, trying to get blootered for the journey.

Everybody on board stared at each other, looking for an explanation for such an outrageous outburst from the captain.

The punters in the aisle seats quickly unclipped their safety belts as they scrambled and climbed unceremoniously over the passengers in the inside seats, to catch a view of the outside from the nearest window.

'I've got a wing on my side!' one guy announced excitedly. 'What about you, hen? Take a look outside. Have you still got a wing on your side?' another frantically enquired. 'Check the tail. See if we still have a tail!'

That short moment seemed like an eternity, and I'm not the only one who was thinking, 'Life belt?'

Equipped with a wee light and whistle to attract attention, and just pull down on the red toggle to inflate it! Well, with all due respect to the crew . . . Fuck right off! I want to pull down on a ripcord hanging from a backpack containing a parachute! I'm jumping out of an aeroplane high up in the sky, not a bloody dinghy in Rouken Glen pond!

In fact, I want two parachutes, just in case the first one doesn't want to open.

Suddenly, the panic and hysteria was interrupted by the intercom as the flight captain's dulcet tones began broadcasting again, announcing to all the passengers the following update:

'Ladies and gentlemen, I would like to express my sincere apologies to any of you on board who might have been upset or frightened by my last broadcast that ended rather abruptly, but while I was speaking to you on the intercom, our new flight attendant Lisa, from Poland, accidentally spilled a piping hot cup of coffee all over my lap.' He paused for a moment before adding, 'You should see the front of my pants!'

At that, a wee Glesca punter sitting behind me shouted, 'The front of your pants? That's fuck all, pal, you should see the back of mine!'

He wasn't alone in that department, as most of the punters formed an orderly queue in the aisle, waiting to use the first available toilet.

Fortunately, peace was restored.

Everybody on board did their utmost to empty the 'trolley dolly' of its offer of 'Bull's Eye' alcohol bags – 'buy one get one free'. 'Gimme six whiskies, doll!' was a popular order.

The offer was made available not because of the air scare, but because trying to open the first bag usually resulted in ripping it the wrong way and spilling most of it all over yourself.

This practice continued even during our descent for landing, and it was no surprise that when we hit the ground so hard that it seemed somewhere along the way we had discarded our landing gear, many passengers never felt it, or heard it above the screams of hysteria!

However, we landed on the runway at Murcia Airport ahead of time, and it was no wonder, considering the amount of excess weight that was 'dumped' down the toilet chute en-route!

The speed of sound could certainly be heard throughout the flight. 'Bbrruupp'!

Or should I say, on behalf of the ladies on board, the smooth turbulence!

As the doors opened to the front and rear of the plane, almost every passenger nervously burst into spontaneous applause on realising we had in fact landed safely.

On passing the cabin crew at the exit door, I couldn't resist. 'Excuse me, Captain, can I ask you a question?'

'Certainly sir!' he replied, eager to please.

'Did you actually land this plane, or were we shot down?'

With that said, I walked down the stairs, while those still on board continued to form a conga line along the passageway en route to the bog.

When they left the plane, it was like something out of the 'Wacky Races' as passengers, dragging cases of hand luggage behind them, made a beeline across the melting tarmac for the security and comfort of the toilets within the terminal building.

Particularly those female passengers who thought it would be a cool idea to travel in their new Primark white linen trousers and thongs. Those stains will never wash out, that's for sure!

Nowadays, just the sight of a Ryanair magazine has the same effect on my bowels as a slug of prescribed 'Lactoluse' from Michelle and the gang at Nigel Kelly the chemist!

Nearly Right, Ma'am!

• • •

Many years ago while attending church, the minister asked during his sermon if anyone in the packed congregation would like to express some praise for prayers that had been answered.

My mother immediately got to her feet and walked forward to the podium where she announced, 'I have a praise I would like to share with you all. Three months ago, my husband, Freddie, was involved in a terrible motorbike accident, whereby his scrotum was completely crushed on impact. The pain he suffered was excruciating and the doctors didn't know if they could help him.'

You could hear muffled groans and gasps from the men in the congregation as they tried to imagine the pain my father had endured.

'Freddie was unable to hold me or his children,' she went on, 'and every move he made caused him terrible pain and suffering.

We prayed as the doctors performed a delicate operation and, fortunately, they were able to piece together the crushed remnants of his scrotum and staple it back into position.'

Again, all the men in the congregation were unnerved and squirmed uncontrollably and uncomfortably in their seats, imagining the painstaking surgery performed on Freddie.

'Now,' she announced in a trembling voice, 'thanks to the power of prayer, Freddie is out of the hospital and the doctors say that, in time, his scrotum should recover completely.'

All the men in the congregation sighed with relief.

The minister got up and tentatively asked if anyone else had anything to say.

At that my dad stood up, walked slowly to the podium, and said, 'I'm Freddie.' The entire congregation held its breath.

'I just want to correct my wife, Flora, and inform the rest of you in here today that it was in fact my sternum!'

Smart Answer

· · ·

A lorry was being driven along a country road when the driver noticed a sign which read: LOW BRIDGE AHEAD.

Before he could take evasive action, the bridge was directly in front of him and he got stuck under it.

Cars were backed up for miles behind him.

Finally, a police motorcyclist arrived. The cop got off his bike, casually walked up to the lorry driver's cab and delivered the obvious line to the driver.

'Got stuck, eh?'

To which the lorry driver nonchalantly replied, 'Not at all, Officer, I'm actually on my way to deliver this bridge!'

Harry's Help Page

· · ·

Dear Harry,

I'm writing to you in the hope that you can help me with my problem.

The other day I set off for work, leaving my husband in the front lounge watching the horse racing as usual. I hadn't driven more than a mile down the road when the engine cut out and my car shuddered to a sudden halt.

Not owning a mobile phone, I had to walk all the way back home in the pouring rain to get my husband's help.

When I arrived at the house I was stunned and shocked to find my husband in our bed with the girl next door.

I am 32, my husband is 34, and the girl neighbour is only 22.

We have been married for twelve years and I never suspected a thing. So when I confronted him about it, he broke down and admitted that he had been having an affair with her for the past three months.

I told him it has to stop, or I will leave him.

Six months ago, due to the credit crunch, he lost his job and has been feeling increasingly depressed and worthless.

I love my husband very much, but ever since I gave him the ultimatum, he has become increasingly distant toward me.

He even refuses to attend counselling sessions with me and I'm afraid I can't seem to get through to him any more.

Please, can you help, Harry?

Sincerely,

Fiona
(True identity withheld)

The Reply

...

Well, Sheila. It is Sheila, isn't it? Let's get straight to the point.

A car stalling after being driven for a very short distance can be caused by a variety of problems with the engine.

Firstly, I would suggest you start by checking that there is no dirt in the fuel line. If it appears clear, then check the vacuum pipes and hoses connected to the intake manifold.

I would also make a check of all grounding wires. If none of these initial approaches solve the problem, then it sounds to me that it might just be the fuel pump itself that's faulty, and as a result of this, it's causing a low delivery of pressure to the carburettor float chamber.

If this is the case, don't waste your time and hard-earned money on a local mechanic charging £30 an hour to look at it!

Trade it in for a new one with a reputable car dealer like Arnold Clark offering 0% interest.

I hope this advice has helped with your problem.

Yours sincerely,

Harry.

PS. Please remember, readers, Harry's Help Page is there to solve all your problems, and Harry's expert advice is provided absolutely free!

Tell Him Anything!

· · ·

One day, on duty at a street gala day with his partner, aptly nicknamed big Blobby, Alex Craig was approached by the local councillor from the area, who had been invited along to perform the opening ceremonies.

During a short chat, he informed them that his new next-door neighbour was a serving police officer, working in the underwater unit.

The councillor was extremely impressed by the fact that his new neighbour had bought and sold several houses within a very short space of time, in order to afford a house in such a select area. It also did not go unnoticed that he had enrolled with the neighbourhood watch, lending his weight and experience behind it.

Quick as a flash, big Blobby informed him that the reason he had moved so many times was not through choice, but because of continual protests and complaints from his neighbours regarding his close relations, who were 'tinkers'.

The councillor was shocked and astounded to hear this information, but beckoned him to continue, and big Blobby was only too pleased to embellish the information he was supplying.

'Well, at least twice a year they come to visit with him and his wife and they arrive in their caravans and trucks, where they set up camp right outside the front of his house.

The worst ones were the Irish bunch that arrived from Dingle. They had a goat and a donkey, which the brood of weans they brought with them would ride up and down the bloody street all day and night to keep them amused. One good point was you could get cheap goat's milk, and if the animals grazed in the garden for free it kept the grass short.

'If I remember right, everywhere they have visited him, the gardens in the area, particularly the roses, benefited from the bags of manure they sold around the doors. Mind you, that's the manure they could be bothered gathering into bags.

'The worst part was it usually took two council tippers the entire week to clear up the rubbish and debris they left, plus the stench from the excess crap deposited by their animals. Phew!

'However, if you're really lucky, it's only twice a year that they come calling. Just arrange your own holidays at that time.'

The councillor was ashen faced, his mouth wide open as he walked off aimlessly, disappearing into the crowd without saying another word after hearing this story – albeit a complete and total fabrication of the truth – by big Blobby.

As for Blobby, he couldn't resist looking straight into Alex's face and saying, 'Was that not a cracker, Alex, eh? Did you see the look on his face? Pure priceless! First time I've seen a councillor stuck for words. He didn't know what to say there. He swallowed the lot, hook, line and sinker!'

We never found out the entire outcome of big Blobby's little chat with the councillor, but we heard it wasn't long after Blobby's chat that our colleague – whom, he admits, was totally unknown to him – had once again moved on up the property ladder.

Or was it down? Glesca polis at their best!

Polis Nicknames

. . .

We used to have an inspector who I personally nicknamed 'Boomerang', because every time I asked him something, he would reply, 'Let me get back to you, Harry!'

Written in Advance

• • •

A recently recruited mature police officer was cited to attend court as a witness for the very first time.

As this was to be his debut in court, he was advised by his more experienced colleagues as to the pitfalls to expect when giving evidence, with regards to traps that defence agents spring on unsuspecting police officers concerning notebook entries.

Forewarned is forearmed, and therefore the mature cop carefully committed his evidence to memory, to ensure all went well.

However, during his evidence, the defence agent asked him if he had made a note of the incident in his notebook.

'Yes sir!' he replied confidently.

He was then asked if he had made the notes at the time of the incident.

To which he replied, rather naively, 'No, I made them shortly before it!'

I'm also informed that on another occasion, a minor embarrassment arose when it was discovered that he had two outstanding warrants against him for non-payment of fines.

After a long interview with the divisional commander, it was discovered that it was a totally innocent misunderstanding.

It appears that when he was completing a Fixed Penalty Notice, instead of noting the offender's details in the section marked Name and Address, he had inadvertently entered his own personal details.

Taking the Piss!

. . .

This is an excerpt from a genuine letter written by an American friend, who is a construction worker.

'I work, they pay me. I pay my taxes and the government distributes my taxes as it sees fit.

'In order to earn my pay cheque, I work on a rig for a construction project.

'As a result, I am required to pass a random urine test, with which I have absolutely no problem.

'However, what I do have a problem with is the distribution of my hard-earned taxes to people who don't have to pass a urine test.

'Shouldn't one have to pass a urine test to get a welfare cheque, because I have to pass one to earn it for them?

'Please understand that I have no problem with helping people get back on their feet, but I do on the other hand have a problem with helping someone sit on their bony ass all day, drinking beer and smoking dope.

'Could you imagine how much money the country would save if all of our people had to pass a urine test in order to qualify for a public assistance cheque?'

Personally, I think he makes a good point – somewhere along the line, someone is definitely taking the piss! What do you think?

Sweaty Betty

...

One night while on beat patrol with Alex Craig, we came across wee Sweaty Betty McColl, the local prozzy of the area.

She was beaming like a Christmas fairy light with a grin from ear to ear and couldn't wait to inform us that she had just left a satisfied punter, after performing her favours up the nearby lane.

'That'll be a first then,' Alex remarked. 'I'm surprised his guide dog wasn't trained to warn him!'

'Very funny, Mr Craig. Turns out he was a new punter on the strip,' she announced excitedly. 'A young guy and gagging for it. So after agreeing tae my price, without any haggling whatsoever, he practically dragged me up the lane.'

While the sexual act was taking place he remarked how she was like a virgin, romantically describing her as being 'tighter than a crab's arse'. That's a new one on me!

He was that pleased, he gave her twenty Woodbine cigarettes, as a tip, with the added promise that he'd return in the future.

'The thing is, little did he know, wi' it being such a cauld night, I was wearing my flesh-coloured tights, and with him in such a rush to get started, I didnae get a chance tae take them aff, and there was no way I was going to upset him by making him wait. The randy big bugger was ready to explode on impact.

'I just patronised him and said he was a big boy for his

age, and that it took me all my time to accommodate him. He was fair chuffed to bits with that compliment.

'So much so that when he left, he was singing Simon and Garfunkel's "Keep the Customer Satisfied" all the way along the road!

'Now, is that no' what you call one happy punter?'

There was absolutely no answer to that one, but then, Sweaty Betty was always exaggerating about something, and it was difficult to know when she was actually telling the truth.

Bath Night
. . .

Whilst my missus and I were bathing my grandson the other night, he grabbed a hold of his testicles and asked, 'Are these my brains, Granny?'

Which prompted her to look straight at me and reply, 'No! Not yet, son. But soon.'

Morris's Text News

. . .

A farmer in Perthshire has made history by growing a field of dildos! Ever since the local paper printed the story, his field has been inundated with squatters!

A recent poll confirmed that 75% of males enjoy having sex in the shower. The other 25% just haven't been to prison yet.

A man arrived home from work one night and caught the gas fitter having sex with his pet dog!

I can't believe the police refused to charge him with bestiality. They said the bastard had an alibi . . . He was corgi registered.

Viagra have just announced a breakthrough in their product. Now available in powder form, you put it in your tea. It does nothing for your erections, but it stops your biscuits going soft!

Doctor John had slept with one of his patients and felt really guilty about it. No matter how much he tried, the sense of betrayal was overwhelming. But every once in a while he'd hear an internal reassuring voice say, 'John, don't worry about it. You aren't the first doctor to sleep with one of your patients and you won't be the last, and after all, you are single, so let it go.'

But invariably the other voice would bring him back to reality, whispering, 'For fuck's sake, John, you're a vet!'

A father of fourteen was shot dead today in Queens Park. Apparently a police marksman mistook him for a rabbit!

There was a big hold-up on the M8 motorway today. Apparently one of those new Skoda cars crashed into a barrier. There were bits of cake, icing and jam everywhere!

The Dentist

· · ·

Having suffered from toothache over the weekend, the first thing on Monday morning I couldn't wait to get to my dentist and have it dealt with.

As I sat there in the chair, under the bright lights, with my head back and mouth wide open, my dentist examined me, after which she advised me that the tooth would have to be extracted.

Reluctantly, I agreed with her decision.

As she prepared to take it out, she said, 'I'll just give you an injection to numb the area.'

'An injection? Oh no you don't! I'm terrified of needles,' I declared.

'Alright then, Harry,' she said. 'I'll administer gas then.'

'Gas? No way! I hate the idea of having a mask over my face. You'll have to give me something else!' I insisted.

At that, she went over to her desk, opened a drawer and took out a small blue pill.

Handing it over to me with a glass of water, she said, 'Here, take this then!'

'What is it, Diane?' I asked her.

'It's Viagra!' she replied.

'Viagra? Will that help take the pain away?' I asked.

To which she replied, 'No, but it will give you something to hold on to when I'm pulling your tooth out!'

Ring Back

. . .

The duty officer of the force control room had endured a busy back shift, overseeing and dealing with numerous calls, including a firearms incident, where he had to obtain ratification for the issuing of firearms from the Deputy Chief Constable, as well as a report of a missing twelve-year-old girl with a learning disability.

About 1.30 a.m. the duty officer was becoming increasingly concerned for the welfare of the missing person, and decided to try ringing her on her mobile phone, using the re-dial facility on the ICCS, a touch-screen communications system, commonly used within most control rooms.

He selected the mobile number and the phone was immediately answered.

Seizing his opportunity to persuade the young girl to return home, he blurted out, 'Carrie! I want you to listen to me. I'm a police officer . . . Please don't say anything, or hang up until I've finished talking. Your mother and father are worried sick about you. Your dad has been driving up and down the M8 looking for you all night. Now listen to me, Carrie, this is really important, it's time you went home.'

There was a slight pause.

'Are you listening to me, Carrie, or am I just talking to myself?'

A male voice then answered, 'No, Carrie isn't listening to you, but you're not talking to yourself!'

'Who is this then?' asked the duty officer rather indignantly.

To which the person on the other end of the phone replied, 'This is the Deputy Chief Constable here, what is it you would like me to ratify for you now, Inspector?'

Gulp!

Smart Answer

· · ·

A police officer operating a radar speed trap stopped a young boy racer for speeding.

He approached the young driver's window and said, 'I've been waiting for you all day, son!'

To which the boy racer replied, 'Well I got here as fast as I could!'

When the cop eventually stopped laughing, he sent the kid on his way, without a ticket.

Erotic Nights

· · ·

Detective Superintendent Beattie was attending a CID course, being organised by the anti-terrorist section of the Metropolitan Police in London.

Having arrived a day early, he checked himself into the hotel, which had been pre-booked for officers attending the course.

Later that evening he began to feel a bit lonely and allowed his mind to stray, as he thought about one of those girls you see advertised in telephone booths when you're calling for a taxi.

He decided to go into a phone booth near the hotel to check for one and immediately found an advertisement for a gorgeous-looking young girl calling herself 'Miss Eroticism', alongside a photograph of a lovely blonde girl bending over a chair.

She had all the right curves in all the right places, beautiful long wavy hair, and long graceful legs all the way up to her oxters – you know the type.

He noted down the telephone number, placed it in his pocket and returned to his hotel.

However, on walking back to his hotel, his guilty conscience took over, resulting in him going straight to his room and retiring to bed for an early night.

The following day, he attended his course at the Met, which was very long and tiring, after which he packed his notes away in his file and was preparing to return to his hotel, when he pulled out Miss Eroticism's phone number from his jacket pocket.

He looked at the number, pondering for a moment, then thought, 'What the hell, I'll give her a call.'

At that he entered a nearby vacant office, picked up the phone, and immediately dialled the number before his conscience kicked in.

'Hello?' the woman answered. She sounded so sexy, he let rip.

'Hi, I hear you give a great all-over body massage, so I'd like you to come over to my room at the Novotel and give me one . . . No, wait, I should be honest with you. I'm only in town for the one night, I'm lonely, and what I really would like is sex. I want it hard! I want it hot! But most of all, I want it right now! I'm talking kinky, the whole night long. You name it, we'll do it. Bring your whip, handcuffs, toys, everything you've got in your bag of tricks. We'll go hot and we'll go heavy! You can tie me up, wear a strap-on, cover me in whipped cream, anything you want, baby, I'm up for it and I have the dosh to pay for it! Now, how does that sound to you?'

There was a moment's pause, then she replied, 'That sounds like it's going to be a fantastic night, sir, but for an outside line you'll need to press nine.'

Beg your Pardon

· · ·

I was down on a visit to my wee mate Malky McCormick's house in Ayrshire, having a cup of coffee and catching up on old times.

Before I knew it, a few hours had elapsed and it was time to head back up the road for home.

As I bid Malky farewell and started driving along the country road, the visibility wasn't very good.

Suddenly, I saw a blue light flashing and got pulled over by a traffic cop for apparently exceeding the speed limit.

'What would you do if Mr Fog came down suddenly?' he asked.

Assuming that he was being sarcastic, I responded in the same manner: 'I would put Mr Foot down on Mr Brake.'

'You obviously misunderstood what I just said. Therefore, let me ask you again, sir,' he said, very condescendingly, before repeating, 'What would you do if MIST or FOG came down suddenly?'

Keep the Tip!

• • •

A lot of retired police officers find it hard to decide what to do after they have left.

However, no such problem for big Donnie Henderson, that well known resident cult figure of the Harry the Polis series of books. Donnie was going to provide the public with an excellent transport service, second to none!

During his first day of providing 'DHS' – or Donnie's Hire Service, as it was better known – he picked up a young girl of about twelve-years-of-age, carrying two big black bin bags. The hire was to convey her to the high-rise flats in Millerfield Road, Dalmarnock, where he would be met by her mother, who would pay him the cost of her fare.

All the way along the road, the young female passenger chatted away to Donnie in a manner very much more mature than her age would suggest.

After almost thirty minutes, Donnie arrived at the destination, but there was no sign of her mother waiting to pay for the hire.

'Toot yer horn, mister, and let her know we're here!' she said.

Donnie carried out his young passenger's instruction, but after several toots and even more minutes had elapsed, there was still no sign of her.

A short time later, after Donnie had intermittently sounded his taxi horn several more times and sat about waiting to be paid for the hire, his young passenger made a suggestion.

'Hey, big man! Let me out and I'll go and get her. It'll speed things up and I'll make sure you get a big tip.'

Donnie thought long and hard about her offer, looking into her wee innocent face, before reluctantly agreeing, but as a guarantee that she would definitely return and not run off, he insisted she leave her two big black bin bags in the back seat of the taxi.

Without the slightest hesitation, she agreed to his request and released her grip on the black bags.

'Now tell your mother to hurry it up, or I'll have to charge for waiting time as well!' he insisted.

'No problem, big man, I'll tell her whit ye said!' replied the young passenger then, as she alighted from the taxi, she added, 'Watch my stuff, be back in a minute!' At that, she disappeared around the other side of the building, out of sight.

Donnie felt quite confident about the situation; having looked into her sweet little innocent face, he was convinced she would return with his money, coupled with the fact, as a guarantee, he had retained her two black bags just in case. Donnie's no' daft!

Five minutes passed . . .

Ten minutes passed . . .

Fifteen minutes passed . . .

Donnie at last began to remember his background as a police officer and suspected that his young passenger was not for making a return appearance with the money she owed him for the fare.

Realising he had been duped by a twelve-year-old sweet little girl, he jumped out of his taxi, opened the rear doors and grabbed the two big bin bags to check out what 'tip' she had left behind.

You can imagine the look on his face when he opened them up, one after another, to discover they were both filled with . . . household rubbish!

Ah well, Donnie, as Loyd Grossman would say, 'The clues were there in the description of the bags.'

Last word on the matter, over to Donnie for his response:

'Ya little bastard!'

Change of Job

• • •

Donnie was telling me that he went along for another job interview as a blacksmith's assistant, after he retired from the police. He was asked if he had ever shoed a horse before.

'No!' replied a confident Donnie. 'But I once told a donkey on Blackpool beach to fuck off! Does that count?'

Begging your Pardon?
...

An elderly couple, who were both widowed, had been going out with each other for a long time.

Urged on by their friends and family, they decided it was finally time to get married.

However, before the wedding, they went out to dinner and had a long conversation regarding how their marriage might work.

They discussed finances, living arrangements, and so on. Finally, the old gentleman decided it was time to discuss the subject of their physical relationship.

'How do you feel about sexual intercourse?' he asked her rather tentatively.

'I would prefer it was infrequently,' she responded.

The old gentleman sat back in his chair for a moment, comported himself, adjusted his spectacles, before leaning over the table and whispering, 'Was that one word, or two?'

Early Retirement Bonus

...

The Army found they had too many officers and decided to offer an early-retirement bonus. They promised any officer who volunteered for retirement an extra bonus of £1,000 for every inch measured in a straight line between any two points in his body.

The officer got to choose what those two points would be.

The first officer to accept asked that he be measured from the top of his head to the tip of his toes.

He was measured at six-feet tall and walked away with a bonus of £72,000.

The second officer to accept was a little smarter and asked to be measured from the tip of his outstretched hands to his toes.

After measuring was completed, he walked out with £96,000.

The third one to apply was a non-commissioned officer, a well-travelled and experienced Sergeant Major, who, when asked where he would like to be measured, replied, 'From the tip of my todger to my testicles.'

It was suggested by the pension man who was measuring that he might want to reconsider, explaining about the nice big cheques that the previous two officers had received. But the old Sergeant Major insisted and they decided to go along with him, providing the measurement was taken by a Chief Medical Officer.

The medical officer duly arrived and instructed the Sergeant Major to 'drop 'em', which he did.

The medical officer moved in and placed the measuring tape on the tip of his todger. Moments later, he stepped back and, looking puzzled, asked, 'Where are your testicles?'

To which the Sergeant Major grinned from ear to ear and blurted out loudly,
'Basra!'

Friendship Between Police

• • •

A policewoman didn't come home one night after her shift. The following morning she told her husband that she had slept over at a friend's house. The husband called his wife's ten best friends, but none of them knew anything about it.

A policeman didn't come home one night after his shift. The following morning he told his wife that he had slept over at a friend's house. The woman called her husband's ten best friends, six of whom confirmed that he had slept over, and four said that he was still there!

Mistaken Identity

· · ·

A city centre branch of Marks & Spencer received a hoax call stating that there was a bomb hidden in the store.

The beat officer for that area was contacted to attend at the store, where they were able to play back the recording of the call.

The officer decided the best way to retrieve the call as evidence was to make a recording from the telephone message, holding a tape recorder in front of the handset.

He contacted his control centre and requested that the duty officer try and locate a Dictaphone and have it brought along to the store in order to record the message.

Several moments later, the officer received a call from the civilian station assistant (a former well respected detective), who informed him that the duty officer force control had instructed him to phone the beat officer at Marks & Spencer ASAP.

The beat cop was slightly confused as to why the station assistant would be contacting him by phone and asked, 'I don't know why you are calling me here, it was a Dictaphone I asked for!'

There was a long period of silence, then the penny dropped – for both of them. 'A dick to phone!'

The beat officer instinctively burst into uncontrollable, hysterical laughter on repeating it several times.

However, the former detective officer on the other end of the phone did not relish the idea of being the butt of the joke, and apparently blurted out some well chosen expletives over the phone at his fellow officer, before abruptly hanging up!

Good Manners
. . .

Just the other day, I was in Morrison supermarket stocking up with the household groceries, and as I approached the check-out, I got there a split second before a frail, respectable-looking elderly woman, who was holding a small carton of milk.

As I started loading up the conveyor belt, my good manners and courteous upbringing took over and I looked at her little pathetic face as she stood there holding her wee carton of milk.

'Is that all you have to put through, hen?' I asked her.

'Yes! Just this quart pint of milk, son,' she replied.

To which I couldn't resist saying, 'Well if I were you, I'd find another check-out, 'cause I'm going to be a while here!'

Alternative Weekend

. . .

A young Glesca boy decided to try his luck down south and moved to London.

The following day, he went to Harrods to apply for a job.

'Do you have any sales experience at this level?' asked Mohammed Al Fayed.

'Experience? Definitely! I worked for five years in the famous Barras market in Glesca,' replied the cocky young Scot.

Mister Al Fayed liked his confident attitude and promptly gave him a job.

The young Scot's first day was busy and challenging, but he got through it.

After the store was closed up for the day, Mister Al Fayed came to see how he was settling into the job.

'So . . . How many sales did you make for me today?' he asked, smiling over at the boy.

The young lad replied, 'Jist the wan, Alfay!'

Mister Al Fayed immediately displayed his disappointment and said, 'What? Just the one sale? I expect my sales people to average between twenty to thirty sales a day! That disappoints me. So how much was the sale for, anyway?'

One hundred and ten thousand, four hundred and thirty-five pounds and fifty pence!' said the boy.

Al Fayed gulped, 'One hundred and ten thousand, four hundred and thirty-five pounds and fifty pence! What did you sell him?'

'Well, firstly ah selt him a wee fish hook, then a medium fish hook, then a fishing rod tae put the hook on tae. Then ah asked him where he was gaun fishing, and he said doon the coast, so ah telt him he wid need a boat for that.

'So ah took him doon tae the boat department and selt him a twin-engined Benetti. Then he said that he didnae think his wee Ford Escort could tow it, so ah took him alang tae car sales and selt him a nice four-by-four Mitsubishi Shogun TDi, wi' Sat Nav, iPod and a few other extras.'

Mister Al Fayed was speechless for a moment.

'Wait a minute. Are you telling me that a customer came in here today to buy a small fish hook, and you convinced him into buying a twin-engine speed boat and a four-by-four Mitsubishi Shogun TDi?'

'Naw! Naw! Naw, Alfay . . . He came in tae buy a box of tampons for his missus, and Ah said, "Well, pal, seein' as how yer weekend's ruined, ye might as well go fishing!'

New Breed

...

Today I was introduced to a brand-new polis straight out the box, as we say.

He is forty-three years of age and a redundant bank employee.

He showed me his induction letter and informed me that he has already been measured for his stab-proof vest and his utility belt, with PR24 baton, CS gas spray, hand-cuffs, pouches, etc.

It's only my opinion, but I would question if this guy has ever seen an angry man in his life, apart from the everyday bank customer who came into the bank to argue the point about incurring bank charges on their account.

At forty-three years of age, I question his sanity to join such a demanding job, because he is not streetwise. But I wholeheartedly applaud his eagerness to find employment, albeit somewhat different from his previous career.

His reward for doing so is that he will be given a full police pension of twenty-five years' service.

If this mature new polis doesn't keep up his fitness, we could be seeing a change in trend, with the police clothing store issuing a walking stick, or even a Zimmer frame to assist him in pounding the beat.

Who knows, he may even be issued with his own patrol battery-operated wheelchair, fitted out with illuminated go-faster stripes and a blue flashing light!

However, he was totally adamant that the public could 'bank' on him with complete confidence!

I just hope and pray that after his three-month stint at the Tulliallan training college, he does not decide to 'withdraw his services and lose interest'!

Case Solved

· · ·

The college commandant called all the recruits together on the parade square and announced, 'I must tell you all something. We have a new case of gonorrhoea in the police college.'

'Thank God for that,' remarked an elderly drill instructor. 'I'm fed up drinking that Merlot crap!'

The Robbery

• • •

A robber burst into a bank wearing a black balaclava over his face and wielding a handgun above his head.

Once inside, he shouted, 'This is a hold up! Everybody get on the floor. Now!'

He then jumped over the tellers' counter and proceeded to empty the cash drawers and stuff the money into his bag.

When finished, he made for the exit door to getaway, when a brave customer jumped up from the floor and tackled him, yanking off his balaclava in the process and exposing his face.

The bank robber immediately turned his gun on the customer and shot him in the head.

He then shouted out to the other customers on the bank floor: 'Did anybody else in here see my face?'

There was total silence, but the robber noticed another customer peering from behind a counter and promptly walked over and shot him in the head, too.

There was screaming and wailing in the bank from some of the other customers on the floor, as they realised what had happened.

Unperturbed by his drastic action – or the consequences – the robber repeated his question.

'Did anybody else see my face?' He recklessly waved his gun around in a threatening manner.

There was absolute silence for a moment, before an elderly male voice was heard calling out from a distant corner of the bank.

'Excuse me, sir, but I think my missus caught a glimpse of you!'

Diarrhoea!

• • •

I must admit that in the beginning, I didn't look forward to performing my stint of desk duties, but due to recovering from a serious back injury, I soon settled into the role of having to deal with the public over the phone and handing out my expert advice on how to deal with their particular complaint, without the need for a police officer to attend at their home address.

I think it might have been the blue light outside the entrance to the police station, but in hindsight, I think it was probably just me! If there was a crackpot, a drunk, a nutcase, a joker, or an aggressive housewife out there, then I was the resident target for all their verbal abuse.

However, I did enjoy some great laughs from the crank calls, anonymous complainers and downright housing scheme comedians, who would regularly call me up when I was on duty.

Such was the case of the following call I received from a lady who sounded rather posh and sophisticated with a polite accent and who would become a welcome regular, with her calls.

'Strathclyde Police, can I help you?'

The caller immediately responded with the following parody: 'Diarrhoea! Diarrhoea! Some people think it's funny, but it's really rather runny. Diarrhoea! Diarrhoea!'

She then replaced the phone. This was one of many parodies she would relate to me anonymously over the phone.

Personally, I thought it was hilarious, because I always thought it ran in your family, but apparently it runs in your genes.

Pray for me!

...

Tommy went along to the church on Sunday night to listen to a black American preacher giving a revival sermon.

After he had finished his sermon, the preacher asked that if anyone present within the congregation needed to be prayed over, they should come forward to the front of the altar.

Tommy got up from his seat and joined the long conga line in the aisle leading to the front.

When it was his turn, the preacher asked, 'Heh, brother, what do you want me to pray about for you?'

Tommy replied, 'Well, preacher, I need you to pray for my hearing.'

The preacher put one finger in Tommy's ear, and placed his other hand on top of his head. At that, he began to pray and pray and pray.

After a few minutes, the preacher removed his hands, stepped back, looked into Tommy's eyes and asked, 'Okay, brother, tell me, how's your hearing now?'

Tommy looked at him with a puzzled expression on his face and replied, 'I don't really know, man, I'm no' due to appear until Tuesday!'

Daddy's on the Phone

. . .

This story cracked me up when I was told it by a friend at a night out.

It's based on a telephone call from a detective officer, while away from home attending a CID course.

Ring, Ring! Ring, Ring!

'Hello?'

'Hi, honey. It's Daddy here. Is Mummy near the phone?'

'No, Daddy. She's upstairs in the bedroom with Uncle Paul.'

After a brief pause, he says, 'But honey, you haven't got an Uncle Paul.'

'Oh yes I have, and he's upstairs in your bedroom with Mummy, right now.'

There's a brief pause while he digests this information and ponders over what to do.

'Okay then, honey, this is what to do. I want you to put the phone down on the table, run upstairs and knock loudly on the bedroom door and shout as loud as you can that Daddy's car just pulled into the driveway.'

'Okay, Daddy, I'll just go and do it.'

At that, she put the phone down and ran up the stairs to the bedroom. A few minutes later, the little girl came back down and picked up the phone.

'I did it, Daddy, I told her.'

'And what happened, honey?' he asked.

'Well, Mummy got such a fright that she jumped out of bed with no clothes on and ran around the room screaming. Then she tripped over the rug and hit her head on the dresser. Now she isn't moving at all!'

'Oh my God! That sounds terrible. What about Uncle Paul. What did he do?' he asked.

'Well! Uncle Paul jumped out the bed with no clothes on, too. He was looking very scared, before he jumped out the back window and into the swimming pool. But I guess he didn't notice that you took out all the water last weekend to clean it. Thud!

'He hit the bottom of the pool and now he isn't moving either. I think he might be dead.'

There was a long pause.

Followed by another long pause.

Then, there was a longer pause.

Followed by an even longer pause.

Then the detective officer says, 'Swimming pool? Is this 01292 . . . ?'

The Horth Whithperer

· · ·

The chief inspector of the police mounted branch called up the stables and informed the duty inspector that a new RSPCA inspector was coming over to inspect the condition of the horses.

'How will I recognise him?' asked the inspector.

'That's easy. He's a wee midget with a speech impediment.'

A short time later, he arrived at the stables and the inspector led him around to look at the horses. He stopped and asked to examine one, so the inspector showed him to their prized mare.

'Nith lookin' horth. Can I thee her eyth?'

The inspector lifted him up and he gave the horse's eyes the once over. 'Nith eyth. Can I thee her earzth?'

The inspector lifted him up again and he checked out the horse's ears. 'Nith earzth. Can I thee her mouf?'

The inspector was becoming fed up with him, but he picked him up again and showed him the horse's mouth. 'Nith mouf. Can I see her twat?'

Totally pissed off by this time, the inspector picked him up and stuck his head as far as he could up the horse's backside, pulled him out and promptly plopped him down on the ground.

At which point the midget got up from the ground, coughing, spluttering and wiping poo from his face and said, 'Perhapth I should have made mythelf clearer . . . When I said twat, I meant, can I thee her wunning awound the stables a widdlebit?'

Cage Rage

· · ·

An urgent call was received to attend the International Bar regarding a disturbance and officers requiring assistance.

Bob Pollok and I attended in the divisional land rover, Delta Seven.

On our arrival, my colleagues Derek Connelly and John Paton were struggling on the floor with a large ned, who was violently resisting arrest, having previously challenged and beaten up several of the patrons within the bar.

We immediately joined in and with considerable difficulty managed to restrain him with handcuffs, after which we all frogmarched him unceremoniously outside and into the rear of the land rover, where we then secured him to the fixed metal wire cage partition of our police vehicle.

Whilst performing this manoeuvre, the bar staff came running outside to inform us that another disturbance was about to start.

All four of us rushed back inside and, after a few moments, we were able to identify those responsible and convince them that it was in their best interest to leave the premises under their own steam, with a police warning.

Moments later, having obtained the necessary statements we required for our report, we left the bar and returned to the land rover, in order to convey our prisoner to the Gorbals station.

However, on our return, we were stunned to find our prisoner was missing, along with the five feet of wire metal grille that he was attached to with the use of police handcuffs.

A lookout was broadcast over the radio and a complete and thorough search was made of the area for our ned, 'Metal Micky', handcuffed and attached to five feet of wire railing.

Surely he would stand out, in Glesca, wearing a metal railing?

Even the local scrap yards were checked, with no trace found.

Moral of the story: 'Sometimes, you should consider using your discretion and give out a police warning'!

Check In
...

The Chief Inspector called for me to come to his office.

'Do you want to see me, sir?' I asked.

'Yes, Harry. Can I ask you a couple of questions?' he said.

'Certainly, sir. So what was your second one?'

Russian Mafia

· · ·

During one of my many tours to Russia, with the Scottish folk band I performed with, we had occasion to be staying at the Sports Hotel, Moscow.

Now this particular hotel had been built for the 1980 Olympics, and as nice as it might have been then, twenty years later, it had been allowed to deteriorate. For example, when you entered the en-suite in your room there were more tiles in the bath than there were still affixed to the walls.

The bed sheets were no bigger than a cotton dish towel and what pile that was left in the carpets, was usually stuck to your feet in the morning.

Breakfast was available daily within the dining area in the basement, but your everyday bacon and egg, or plain continental breakfast, was definitely nowhere to be seen.

As for the waiting staff, none of them would have looked out of place in the Michael Jackson video, *Thriller*. And they would have saved money on the make-up.

During my three-week stay, while touring with the band, I only ever made the one visit to the dining room, and even that seemed like one visit too many and resembled a scene from the *Rocky Horror Show* as they appeared in a line ready to perform the 'Time Warp'! Come to think of it, several waitresses looked suspiciously like Richard O'Brien's hump-backed character.

However, as luck would have it, on our floor there was a small bar/lounge, where we enjoyed some great nights celebrating, after returning from our concert performances.

The bar was run by a Ukrainian woman called Natasha, who worked, ate and slept in a small room at the rear of the bar, which enabled her to save some money and send as much as she could afford back to her husband and two children, who remained at home, back in the Ukraine.

Natasha was something of a mother figure to us all, so in order to provide her with some extra money, we gave her an impromptu 'Fanny Craddock' lesson – not on how to make donuts, but how to make French toast, with simple slices of bread, soaked in milk and egg, then fried in a pan.

She would prepare this every morning for us. The only thing was, she never knew when to stop and we had to repeatedly tell her, 'Enough Natasha, enough!' as she continued to produce plate after plate of stacked up slices of toast, until it was coming out of our ears, with the occasional plate or two being skimmed out the windows like frisbees, out of her view, so as not to offend her.

One particular night we arrived back to find the bar area somewhat busier than usual with several young Scots in kilts. It transpired that they were part of the Dumbartonshire drum and pipe band, who had arrived earlier that evening to take part in the Moscow Highland Games.

They had all been sitting around a large table, drinking beers with their pipe major Morven, an attractive blonde lady, when a few of the locals decided to push their way into the company, closing in on Morven.

The relief on their faces was there for all to see when we walked into the bar, for most of the Dumbarton band members were teenagers and were being intimidated by the nasty-looking Russian locals.

The band immediately introduced themselves to us and, before very long, we were competing with our aggressive hosts for the seats around the table, and in particular, the ones on either side of Morven.

It wasn't long before I had managed to wedge myself into a seat, squeezing myself between Morven and this balding, macho male, who was intent on putting his unwanted arm around her.

I immediately introduced myself to him as her husband, using subtlety to warn him off and to stop annoying her.

Unfortunately, all I did was turn the heat onto myself as he sat beside me, staring menacingly, creating an uncomfortable tension around the table.

In an attempt to defuse the situation, I stood up and pointed for him to come to the bar, but I think my action was misinterpreted, as this seven-feet tall Russian giant arose from a chair behind me and, ever so gently, sat me back down into my chair.

He then appeared with two bottles of beer, which he locked together and pulled apart, flicking the tops off both at the same time. He handed me one.

Moments later, my staring Russian nudged my arm, produced an open wallet for a brief moment and said, 'Mafia!'

I couldn't resist saying, 'You're Mafia? My arse.' Confident they weren't recruiting midgets from the Early Learning Centre.

He again produced his wallet, opening it for a split second, this time long enough for me to identify the Russian spelling for police. I said, 'You are Mafia?'

To which he nodded and pointed to his chest. 'Mafia!'

I then signalled for him to stay seated, while I went along to my room. When I returned, I sat down beside him, flashed my police warrant card and said, 'Me Mafia! Scottish Police Mafia!'

He looked intently at my warrant card and a wry smile slowly broke out across his face.

He then spoke to his giant minder, who produced two glasses, which he poured vodka into, and toasted me in Russian as we drank it down. More vodka was poured and I toasted him.

Before I could say 'Crackerjack' he had removed his gold Rolex watch and was trying to fit it onto my wrist.

Next, he removed his fancy buckled belt. 'You like my belt?' He gave me it. 'My shoes, real crocodile skin, here, you take my shoes.' He couldn't give me enough.

As it was, the shoes were about a size six, made for a small boy, so rather than amputate half my foot, I let him keep them along with the belt, but I did hold on to the gold Rolex watch. I'm not that daft!

Mind you, the bloody watch turned out to be a fake just like him. 'Russian Mafia! Trained exclusively by Mothercare!'

Retired Cops' Reunion

• • •

Three mischievous old retired cops were sitting on a bench outside the police convalescent home when an ex-policewoman walked by.

One of the old cops yelled out: 'We'll bet you anything you want, we can tell exactly how old you are.'

The elderly policewoman said, 'You lot would struggle to remember your own names, never mind my age, so there is absolutely no bloody way that any of you lot can guess my age. You're just a bunch of old fools.'

One of the old cops responded, 'Sure we can! Just you lift your skirt up and drop your pants and we'll tell your exact age.'

'Aye right! So you will, ya bunch of perverts!' she replied.

'No, genuine, we're being serious,' another said.

Embarrassed just a little at their request, but anxious to prove they couldn't do it, she lifted up her skirt and dropped her drawers to the floor.

The old cops asked her to turn around a couple of times and then to jump up and down several times in front of them.

She carried out their request for a few moments, turning around and jumping up and down, then said, 'Right, ya shower of dirty old buggers, go for it. What's my age?'

At that, they all piped up and said, 'You're exactly seventy-seven years old!'

Standing there, still holding her skirt up, with her pants

down around her ankles, the elderly policewoman asked, 'So how the hell did you lot manage to guess that?'

Slapping their knees and grinning from ear to ear, the three old cops happily yelled out in unison: 'Cause we were all at your birthday party earlier!'

No-Frills Meals

• • •

It was mealtime during the miners' strike at Ravenscraig.

The canteen lassie, a blatant sympathiser of the miners' cause, asked a young cop in the front of the queue: 'Would you like a meal, sir?'

The young cop asked her, 'What are my choices?'

Totally disgusted with the entire situation, she replied, 'Yes or No!'

The Ultimate Test

• • •

So tell me . . . Just how would you have done then?

Fraser was a happy young police probationer. He had been dating his gorgeous policewoman girlfriend for over a year, and they both decided it was time to get married. There was only one thing bothering Fraser . . .

Her stunningly beautiful younger sister.

His prospective sister-in-law was twenty-three, had long blonde hair, stunning good looks and wore very tight miniskirts.

Also, it did not go unnoticed by Fraser that she generally walked around the house completely bra-less.

She would regularly bend down when she was near him, and would afford him more than a nice view of her butt.

There was no way her actions were mere coincidence. It had to be deliberate, because it was most noticeable to Fraser that she never did it when next to anyone else.

One particular day, the younger sister called Fraser and asked him to come over and check the wedding invitations.

When Fraser arrived at the house, she was alone and she whispered seductively in his ear that she had feelings and desires for him that she couldn't overcome.

She also suggested that she was available, if he wanted to have her just once, before he got married and committed his life forever, to her sister.

Well, Fraser was in total shock and couldn't say a word.

She then said, 'I'm going upstairs to my bedroom, and if you want to have your evil way with me, just come up and get me.'

Fraser was stunned and somewhat gob-smacked at her blatant, provocative open invitation.

Numb and in total shock, he watched her as she slowly climbed the stairs leading to her bedroom.

He pondered over what had been suggested to him, trying to digest exactly what he was being offered, while wrestling with his emotions.

Suddenly, he turned and made a beeline for the front door and ran outside.

Once outside, he headed straight towards his parked car.

Lo and behold, to his surprise, his entire future family were standing outside, at which point they all began to applaud his actions.

With tears in his eyes, his future father-in-law hugged him tightly to his chest and said, 'Fraser, we're so happy that you have passed our little temptation test. We couldn't have asked for a better man to marry our daughter. Welcome to the family, son!'

And the moral of this story is: 'Sometimes it pays to keep your condoms in the glove compartment of the car!'

You Decide!
· · ·

This is a wee test which only has one question, but it's a very important one. By giving an honest answer, you will discover where you stand morally.

THE SCENARIO
You are in Scotland – Glasgow to be specific. There is chaos all around you, caused by a hurricane with severe flooding. This is a flood of biblical proportions.

You are a photo-journalist working for a major daily newspaper, and you're caught in the middle of this epic disaster. The situation is nearly hopeless. You're trying to shoot career-making photos. There are houses and people swirling around you, some disappearing before your eyes, into the overflowing River Clyde.

Nature is unleashing all of its destructive fury at once.

THE CHOICE
Suddenly, you see a man in the river. He is frantically fighting for his life, and trying not to be taken down with the debris.

You move closer. Somehow, the man looks familiar.

Suddenly you realise who it is – George Galloway!

You are aware that the raging waters of the River Clyde are about to take him down under forever.

You are rapidly tiring from your own exertions, but you have to make a quick decision with only two options available to you.

You can prove your indefatigability (that's easy for you to say) and save the life of George Galloway, or you can shoot a dramatic Pulitzer Prize winning photograph, documenting the death of one of the country's most anti-imperialist men, and swell your bank balance by earning a fortune for it.

THE QUESTION

Here's the question, and please think carefully and give a truly honest answer straight from your heart . . .

Would you select a high-resolution contrast colour film, or would you just go with the classic simplicity of black and white?

Career Change

...

A passenger in a taxi arrived at his destination and leaned forward to tap the driver on the shoulder and pay him the fare.

The driver let out a loud scream, shot forward, lost control of the cab, nearly hit an articulated lorry, drove up over the kerb and stopped just inches away from a large plate-glass window.

For a few moments everything was silent in the cab, then the cab driver said,

'Please, don't ever do that again. You scared the bloody living daylights out of me.'

The passenger, who was also frightened, apologised and said he didn't realise that a tap on the shoulder could frighten him as much as it did.

The driver replied: 'I'm sorry, it's really not your fault at all, but today is my first day driving a cab. I have been driving a hearse for the past twenty-five years.'

Big Burd

...

A lady was picking her way through the frozen turkeys at a branch of Sainsbury's, but she couldn't find one big enough for her family.

She asked my son Scott, 'Excuse me, son, but do these turkeys get any bigger?'

Quick as a flash Scott replied, 'I'm afraid not, missus, they're all dead!'

Rope a Dope

...

A polis card school was taken very seriously during the Friday tea break while working late shift. Being a probationer, you were considered too young to be included, so you watched.

Whilst sitting looking on, the sergeant walked in and called to one of the probationers, 'Lesley, there's a bereaved wife sitting in the front of the office wanting to report the sudden death of her man. Away out and deal with it.'

Les went outside to see the deceased wife and then accompanied her on foot from the Gorbals police station, to her home address in the Oatlands area of Glasgow. En route she explained that her husband, Wee Jimmy, was a regular drunk and every night when he returned home from the pub, he would become very argumentative with her.

This would result in him becoming very aggressive, before getting a kitchen chair out, standing on it, putting the ceiling pulley clothes rope around his neck and carrying out his usual drunken ritual of threatening to hang himself.

The rope was old and had been repaired so many times that when he kicked the chair away, it would inevitably always break under the strain of his body weight.

However, on this particular Friday, the wife had decided to invest in a new rope and asked her next-door neighbour to change it.

Unaware of the latest house improvements carried out

by his wife in his absence, Wee Jimmy performed his usual death-defying 'hangman' leap, but this time the rope didn't break.

Due to Wee Jimmy being a 'dead' weight, she could not lift him up and, anyway, he was wildly kicking out at her as she tried to get near him.

As Les entered the house, sure enough, there was wee Jimmy, blue in the face, still dangling from the ceiling, with the new pulley rope around his neck like a failed bungee jumper.

And the moral of the story is: 'It's not always wise to be a creature of habit because sometimes the change can be deadly!'

Where's the Burd?

...

Having retired from the police service a few years ago, I have continued to keep in touch with an older, senior cop who I worked with during my police probation and who had retired from the job several years before me.

Richard lived alone, and on my occasional visits to his house, accompanied by my wife, being a keen amateur chef, he would make a slap-up meal for us, after which we would sit back with a large brandy and reminisce for hours about old times.

During my last few visits, I had detected Richard was becoming forgetful and acting differently, but I put it down to loneliness, having resided on his own for so long.

As a result, I decided to buy him a pet for some company and, on the advice of the pet-shop owner, purchased a mature parrot.

Having paid for the parrot, I arranged for the pet-shop owner to deliver it to Richard's home address as a surprise for him.

A few days later Richard was visiting my house and I asked him if he enjoyed the surprise delivery of the bird.

Richard looked straight into my eyes and said with a smile creasing his face, 'I loved it! In fact, I even had enough left to make sandwiches the following day!'

My mouth fell open in total shock at this announcement.

My wife couldn't contain herself and rushed out of the room.

I stood there in front of Richard, looking at him and trying to think of what to say, while he sat there looking back at me with this innocent smile on his face. Then Richard broke the silence and said, 'You should see your face! You really believed me there!'

At that, we both burst out laughing. Him with the satisfaction of winding me up, and me with sheer relief that he was only joking!

The Traffic Jam

· · ·

Early one morning, along with Graham 'Povie' Edward, I was directed to attend a road accident in Hope Street in Glasgow.

On our arrival, the beat cop Andy Stewart was in attendance, directing the traffic, with other cops looking on.

The accident involved a baker's van that had shed part of its load of pallets containing cream, jam, strawberry buns and doughnuts across the roadway.

Graham, being the senior cop, immediately took control of the situation and began instructing the other cops present.

While he was doing this, I noticed that Andy Stewart was hiding a doughnut behind his back, which he threw at me.

On seeing him throw it, I took evasive action and ducked, whereby it struck Graham full in the face.

Graham slowly wiped the cream from his face, bent down, picked up a bun and let fly at Andy, striking him on the back.

When it hit the target, everybody joined in and a tit-for-tat battle ensued among all the cops present, with cream buns and jam doughnuts flying about everywhere, until we ran out of fresh ammunition.

The entire junction, along with every polis involved, was covered head to toe in cream and jam.

Graham quickly made a call to the bakery, with the promise that their driver would not be prosecuted if the remaining doughnuts left in the van were donated to the Glesca polis.

This agreed, the cleansing department were contacted and a share out was arranged with them, to clean the street and shop windows, while we sorted out the traffic 'jam'!

The remaining doughnuts were shared with the night shift.

Don't ever let anyone say that we in the City of Glasgow Police didn't take our job seriously!

Debt to Society

. . .

Now some people are really stupid! So be sure and cancel your credit cards before you die, particularly if you don't want your next of kin encountering the following scenario with the bank customer services.

A few weeks after an elderly lady died, the bank where she had her current account billed her for February and March, in their annual service charges, for possessing a credit card. They then added salt to the wound by claiming late fees and interest on the monthly charge.

The balance had been £0 when she died, but had now accumulated around £60. As a result of this charge, a family member placed a call to the bank.

Here is the exchange of words that took place:

Family Member: 'I am calling to tell you she died back in January.'

Customer Service: 'Well I'm afraid the account was never closed and as a result of that the late fees and charges still apply.'

Family Member: 'Maybe you should hand it over to a debt collection agency.'

Customer Service: 'Since it is two months overdue, we already have.'

Family Member: 'So, what will they do when they find out that she is dead?'

Customer Service: 'We will either report her account to the frauds division, or report her to the credit bureau, maybe both!'

Family Member: 'Don't you think God might be extremely mad at her?'

Customer Service: 'I beg your pardon?'

Family Member: 'Did you hear what I just told you about her being dead?'

Customer Services: 'Sir, I think you'll have to speak to my supervisor.'

The Supervisor comes on the phone.

Family Member: 'I'm calling to inform you that my aunt died back in January with a zero bank balance.'

Customer Service: 'Well I'm afraid her account was never closed down and the late fees and bank charges still apply.'

Family Member: 'So you want to collect from her estate?'

Customer Service: (Stammer) 'Are you her lawyer?'

Family Member: 'No, I'm her nephew and next of kin.'

Customer Service: 'Could you fax us the death certificate?'

Family Member: 'If it will resolve the matter, yes.'

After the bank received the fax:

Customer Services: 'I'm sorry, but our system just isn't set up to deal with a family death. So I don't know what more I can do to help you.'

Family Member: 'Well, if you manage to figure it out manually, great! But if not, you could just keep billing her. She won't really give a toss.'

Customer Service: 'Well, I'm sorry to hear you taking that attitude, but the late fees and charges still apply.'

Family Member: 'Would you like to make a note of her change of address for future correspondence from the bank?'

Customer Services: 'That would certainly help.'

Family Member: 'Okay, it's Cardonald Memorial Cemetery, Berryknowes Road, Glasgow. Plot number sixty-nine.'

Customer Service: 'Excuse me, sir, but that address you have given me would appear to be a cemetery!'

Family Member: 'That's correct! And what do you do with dead people in your family when they die?'

Customer Services: 'Are you saying that the account holder is genuinely deceased?'

Family Member: 'That is exactly what I'm saying, and if you would like to speak with her personally in the future, I would suggest you do it through Derek Acora or Doris Stokes'!'

Customer Service: 'Are they representing her?'

Family Member: 'I'm afraid there's no hope for you. Goodbye!'

Fancy Dress Party

• • •

A young married couple, both serving police officers, were invited to a fancy dress party.

On the day of the party, the wife suffered a terrible migraine headache and told her husband to go to the party by himself.

Being a devoted husband, he protested, but she argued and said she was going to take some aspirin and retire to her bed early, so there was no need to spoil what would be a good time for him.

So he took the bag with the costume he'd hired for the party and away he went.

After sleeping soundly for about an hour, the wife awakened without pain and, as it was still reasonably early, she decided to go along to the party.

Since her husband did not know what her costume was, she decided she would have some fun by watching her husband and seeing exactly how he behaved when she was not with him.

She joined the party and it didn't take long before she spotted her husband cavorting around on the dance floor, dancing and flirting with every available woman he could, and he wasn't averse to sneaking a little feel here and a little kiss there.

The wife decided it was time to intervene and sidled up to him. Being a rather seductive babe in her costume, he left his current dance partner high and dry to devote some time to the new babe that had just arrived.

She let him go as far as he wanted – after all, it was her husband.

Finally, he whispered a proposition into her ear and she agreed. Off they went to one of the cars parked outside in the driveway, where they engaged in a quickie on the back seat.

Just before the unmasking of everyone at midnight, the wife slipped away, went home, put the costume away and jumped back into bed, to ponder over what kind of explanation her husband would come up with for his deceitful behaviour.

She was sitting up in bed reading when her husband arrived home and walked into the room. She couldn't wait to ask what kind of evening he'd had at the party.

'Oh, just the usual boring old time by myself. You know I never have a good time when you're not there,' he replied.

'Did you dance much then?' she asked.

'Dance? I never even had one dance.
When I got there, I met up with Pete and Bill Brown from my shift, along with some of the other guys, so we disappeared into a spare room and ended up playing poker all evening . . .

'But you're never going to believe what happened to the guy who borrowed my fancy-dress costume!'

What Birthday?

• • •

Gordon called me to say he was in trouble. He'd forgotten about Liz's birthday.

Apparently Liz was furious. She told him, 'Tomorrow morning, Gordon Tourlamain, I expect to find my birthday present in the driveway and the needle better go from zero to a hundred in less than ten seconds – and Gordon, it had better be there!'

The following morning Gordon awoke early, slipped out of bed and left for the office.

When Liz awoke, she looked out of the window and sure enough there was a large coloured box, gift-wrapped and sitting in the middle of the driveway.

Confused by this, she put on her dressing gown and rushed outside to the driveway and brought the large gift box back inside the house.

She ripped open the packaging to find a brand-new set of bathroom scales.

Poor Gordon, he has now been missing since Friday.

I would ask all readers of this book to please pray for his safe return.

Heed Your Speed!

· · ·

Grampian Police were apparently performing a speed radar check, issuing Fixed Penalty Notices to every offender they stopped, when an RAF fighter aeroplane from a local airbase came zooming over the horizon into view.

The police speed radar and camera equipment, to the joy of the officers operating it, registered a speed in excess of 300mph.

However, the sophisticated camera equipment could not be reset afterwards and as a result stopped working, thereby preventing any further speed operations being carried out.

The Chief Constable was not pleased when informed of the damage sustained to their sophisticated police equipment and subsequently fired off a strongly worded letter of complaint to the RAF, pointing out that due to the intervention of one of their jets, target figures had not been attained.

The RAF command promptly replied with their own written correspondence that the radar gun being used by the police officers at that time had been identified by the flight crew of the Tornado aircraft as a hostile weapon and therefore they took immediate, precautionary action by sending a jamming signal back to it.

At the same time, the sidewinder missile was primed and ready for launch as a result of this.

Fortunately – or unfortunately, depending on your point of view – the aircraft pilot overrode the automatic protection system before taking such drastic action.

A few more Tornado fighter aircraft operating within the vicinity of speed camera sites just might prove interesting with regard to target figures *not* being reached!

Oh, and not forgetting the council suffering a large reduction in the amount of lost revenue which they collect on a regular basis from the persecuted motorist.

Confession Time

• • •

A man went to the chapel for confession and said, 'Father, I have sinned. I had sex with five women last night!'

The priest said, 'My son, I want you to go straight home and drink the juice of ten freshly squeezed lemons!'

The man asked if after doing this, would his sins be forgiven?

'No!' replied the priest. 'But it will wipe that frigging smug look off your face!'

Sweet Revenge
. . .

A respectable senior police officer's wife went into the local chemist's shop, walked up to the pharmacist, looked him straight in the eyes and said, 'I would like to purchase cyanide please.'

'What in the world would you want with cyanide?' the pharmacist asked.

'Because I want to poison my husband,' replied the lady.

The pharmacist raised his eyebrows and exclaimed, 'God forgive you, but I can't just hand you cyanide over the counter in order for you to kill your husband; it's against the law. I'd lose my pharmacy licence. Not to mention the fact that they would throw us both in jail! All kinds of bad things could happen here. No, I'm sorry, but absolutely not! I cannot give you cyanide!'

At that, the lady reached into her handbag and pulled out a picture and handed it over to the pharmacist to look at.

The pharmacist took hold of the photograph, viewed it for a moment, then immediately recognised his naked wife in an uncompromising position in bed with the lady's husband.

The pharmacist continued to view the picture for a few moments longer, before responding, 'Now that's different. You forgot to mention the fact that you had a prescription!'

The Note

. . .

The entrance door to the police station was thrown open and in walked a rather disgruntled and irate man.

'Ah'm no' talking tae you, I want tae speak wi' a real polis!' he said to the young female station assistant, who quickly scampered away from the public area to find me and inform me of his demand.

I made my way over to the front desk and instantly recognised the complainer, by the steam emanating from both ears.

'Can I help you sir?' I politely asked.

'Aye ye can that! Ye can trace the bitch that crashed intae my motor while it was parked at the side o' the road and stoved in my front wing and smashed my headlights, before driving aff!'

'Did anybody witness the accident?' I enquired.

'Aye! The whole bloody street saw her dae it, then get out of her fancy car, write a note and pin it under my windscreen wiper for all tae see. Acting as though she was doing the right thing.'

'Oh well, you've cracked then,' I replied, as I turned to grab a Road Accident Form from the cabinet. 'That's what I like to hear, plenty of witnesses and the other driver left full details!'

'Well you'll no' want tae hear this horror story!' he said.

I didn't understand what he meant – lots of witnesses saw her do it and she put a note with her details under his wiper. No!

'Naw, mate! The fly cow got out of her car, said she

couldn't wait as she had tae collect her wean fae school and she would write her details on a piece o' paper and put them on my wiper.

'Not wan bugger thought anything about it, 'cause o' the note, so nae bugger bothered tae take her number as she fucked aff!'

'But what about the note with her details?' I asked him.

'This note?' he replied, handing it over for me to read.

It said: 'Just crashed into your car, people are looking at me, so I'm writing this wee note to fool them. Sorry!'

The Dog

· · ·

A police dog handler was working away in his garage, when he was approached by his young daughter, who asked him, 'Dad, can I take Molly for a walk around the block?'

Now Molly was a Cocker Spaniel police dog that was trained for sniffing out drugs.

Her dad replied, 'No you can't take Molly for a walk around the block, because Molly is in season!'

'What does that mean?' she innocently asked.

'It means she has to be kept on her lead,' he replied.

'But I promise I'll keep her on a lead, Dad.'

He paused for a moment while considering, then said, 'Right, but bring her over here first.'

At that, he took an oily cloth, soaked it in petrol and scrubbed Molly's backside with it, in order to try and disguise the scent of being in season.

'Ok, you can take her for a walk now, but remember, you must keep her on a tight leash, and only go the once around the block!'

'Off went his daughter with Molly restrained at the end of a leash.

Several minutes later she appeared back at the garage without Molly.

'Where's Molly?' her dad asked with concern in his voice.

To which his young daughter replied, 'She ran out of petrol about halfway round the block, so another dog is helping to push her back home!'

Ann Summers' Condiments

• • •

A man and woman CID police officers engaged on escort duty were sitting beside each other in an aeroplane, en route to London.

The policewoman sneezed, took out a paper tissue and gently wiped her nose, before visibly shuddering for ten to fifteen seconds.

The male police officer went back to reading the terms of the warrant.

A few minutes later, the policewoman sneezed again, took a paper tissue, wiped her nose, and then shuddered violently once more.

Assuming that his female colleague might have the start of a cold, he was curious about the shuddering.

After a few more minutes had passed, the policewoman sneezed yet again and, just as before, she took a tissue, wiped her nose, then her body began shaking even more than before.

Puzzled by her actions and unable to restrain his curiosity, he said, 'I couldn't help but notice that each time you've sneezed, you've wiped your nose, and then shuddered violently in your seat. Are you alright?'

'I'm so sorry if I've disturbed you, but I have a very rare medical condition. Whenever I sneeze, it brings on an orgasm.'

Her colleague, more than a little bit embarrassed, was still very curious and said, 'I have never heard of anyone with that condition before. Are you taking anything for it?'

To which the policewoman replied, 'Aye. Lots and lots of ground black pepper!'

Old Age is Fun

· · ·

Serving police officers frequently ask retired police officers what they do to make their days interesting.

Well, let me provide you with an example of my average day.

On Tuesday, the wife and I went into Glasgow city centre and went into a coffee shop. We were only in there for a short while, but when we came back outside, there was a Traffic Warden writing out a parking ticket.

We approached him and said, 'Come on, man, how about giving a former police officer and senior citizen a break?'

He totally ignored us and continued writing out the ticket.

I couldn't contain myself and called him a big fascist bastard.

He glared at me and said, 'Good one, sir!' as he promptly issued another Fixed Penalty ticket for worn tyres.

At that, my wife felt compelled to join in and referred to him as a dirty big bully, who should be wearing Nazi uniform and black leather jackboots.

This prompted an angry response as he finished writing the second ticket and put it on the windshield alongside the first one and said, 'Keep it up, both of you! I have a full book here.' Then, opening his ticket book at another fresh page, he began writing out a third penalty ticket.

This response from the Traffic Warden continued for a further twenty minutes, and the more abuse we directed at him, the more offences he detected with the car, and as a result, the more Fixed Penalty tickets he affixed to the windscreen.

Personally, we couldn't have cared less, because we both travelled into town by public transport, using our new bus passes.

Being retired now for several years, we try our best to have a little bit of fun each day. After all, it's important at our age to keep our mind occupied and prevent boredom creeping in!

The Twenty Pound Note

. . .

My cousin and his wife decided to have a romantic night out at the local cinema.

Being very unsteady on his feet and requiring the use of a walking aid, they timed it to perfection, as the last couple in the queue were disappearing inside.

As he shuffled forward to the ticket kiosk, he looked down and saw a crisp £20 note on the floor. Unable to bend down and pick it up himself, he promptly covered it with his foot.

Turning to his wife he said, 'Jean, I'm standing on a twenty-pound note. Bend down as if you're tying my shoe lace, pick it up, put in your bag and it'll pay for our fish supper when we come out of the cinema!'

Jean said, 'I haven't got my bag with me.'

'Well, put it in your purse then!'

'I've left my purse in the car!' she replied.

'Well put it anywhere, but hurry up before somebody else sees it,' Jack said, getting irate.

Jean bent down and as he moved his foot to the side, she quickly grabbed it and hid it from sight.

'Where did you put it?'

'I've put it down the front of my knickers!' she said.

They both entered the cinema and took their seats for the start of the film, totally satisfied with their find.

At the end of the film, they were walking back to the car when Jack said, 'Right, Jean, get the twenty pounds out for the suppers.'

Jean looked at him and replied, 'I'm sorry, Jack, but it's gone!'

Jack stared at her with a puzzled look on his face and said, 'You put it down the front of your knickers!'

To which Jean responded rather meekly, 'I know! But I didn't realise the man sitting next to me was a thief!'

The Adventures of Harry the Polis

* * *

Some advice for the professional 'Glesca' ned out there.
Here's a wee tip for all you budding neds out there, hoping
for a successful career in crime. If at any time you find yourself in the position where you are being chased by a bloody
big police dog, try not to run through a tunnel, climb up
onto a little seesaw, or jump through a hoop of fire.

Why? I hear you ask, keen to know.

Because they're trained for that, ya silly buggers!!

Enquiry for a gig!
I received a phone call last night to do a live gig at a fire
station. So I made my way along to the location, only to
find out that it was a bloody hoax call!!

During the Police Scot Exams.
Police Examiner: 'Harry, I can't help but notice your
composition on 'A Strathclyde Police Dog' is exactly, word
for word, the same as the person sitting next to you. Did
you copy his essay?'

Harry: 'I certainly did not, sir! It just so happens we
were both writing about the same police dog!'

During a course lecture at the Police College.
My shift inspector once posed a question to me while
filling out his newspaper crossword. He asked, 'Harry,
what do you call a person who continues to talk when
people are no longer interested in listening to him?'

I immediately responded with, 'Inspector?'

Polis Don't Lie!

...

Big Willie McGuire was the local beat officer for the Saltmarket area of Glasgow and, being the newly appointed probationer to the shift, Donnie was instructed to meet up with Willie at Glasgow Cross, as he was performing nightshift overtime.

Donnie was to meet the bus coming from Springburn with Willie on board, en route from a house party, and was given the added responsibility of making sure Willie was sober enough to perform his extra duties.

After meeting up, they were directed to attend a call in the Saltmarket regarding a domestic dispute.

On their arrival at the house, the son was drunk and verbally abusing his mother, because she had never informed him of the true identity of his real father.

Willie immediately intervened and said to the son, 'Don't you dare speak to your mother like that again, or even attempt to insult your father.'

The son looked up at big Willie standing there, towering over him, and loudly gulped, as he digested what Willie had said.

Suffice to say, the son was totally speechless at this impromptu announcement by a big Glesca polis in uniform.

The following day, when Willie took up his beat duty, he discovered a quarter bottle of whisky and two cans of Guinness had been left in the Saltmarket police signal box for him, with a note: 'TO DAD'.

Donnie was never called back to the house ever again.

However, he often wonders if big Willie was using clever Glesca Polis tactics to defuse a situation that night, or was he actually revealing the possible truth?

Play Around

• • •

One day, a police officer came home from work and was greeted by his wife dressed in a very sexy Ann Summers see-through nightie.

'Tie me up, darling!' she purred excitedly. 'And I'll let you do anything you want.'

So he tied her up like she asked and then went off to play a round of golf.

Private Health

...

In this day and age, private health insurance would appear to be the way to go.

Midway through my police service, I was advised to take out PHI with BUPA. 'You'll never regret it!' I was told by the many police officers who succumbed to this advice before me.

Being of good health and one who played a lot of sports and exercised regularly, I was hesitant, but decided to join it, since the police were being given a discounted price to enrol.

I have only ever used the facilities on offer by BUPA on very rare occasions, but have noticed a large increase in my monthly subscription charges over the last few years.

Therefore, having sat down one day and looked at the total cost of my private healthcare policy, I reckon the only way I'm going to break even, or recuperate some of my expenditure before I vacate this world for good, is to have the following list of ailments and the subsequent treatment recommended by my GP and authorised by BUPA:

Open heart surgery, a kidney transplant, two hip replacement operations, a new knee cap, laser eye surgery, four colonoscopies, two colonic irrigation sessions, circumcision of my penis, three cartilage operations, the removal of my appendix, two hernias, the removal of a suspicious mole on my back, tonsillitis, followed by daily sessions of physiotherapy for the next three years – oh, and a six-week stint in the Priory Clinic for alcohol and drug abuse!

By the way, I've just heard there is a new Viagra treatment on the market which you can buy from the local Glesca pharmacy in a bottle and administer it in the same way as you do Optrex eye drops.

It doesn't give you an erection, but it makes you look hard!

D. I. Y. TVs

· · ·

I received a call one day to attend a complaint regarding a loud bang heard coming from the house of Usuf, in the Govanhill area of Glasgow.

Along with my colleague Joe Doris, I made my way to the address which was situated two stairs up in a tenement close.

We knocked on the door, which was answered by a small Turkish man, who invited us inside.

Once inside we explained why we were there and if he could explain to us what the loud bang was.

Mister Usuf then led us over to a sad-looking Bush television in the corner and said it had blown up when he switched it on.

As he removed the back of the TV to show us, I noticed that it was smoking and burnt in appearance inside, but after further inspection, I noticed several of the valves were different bright colours.

I looked over at a table in the room and saw six or seven small Airfix aeroplane model paint pots.

I then turned my attention back to Mister Usuf and asked him what he had done to cause the television to blow up.

He replied in his broken English: 'I am deciding that I want to change it from black and white, to a colour TV. So I have been painting the valves with my many colours. After I'm finishing, I'm switching it on to check if the colours was right . . . and BOOM! There was a big sparky bright flash and smoke from the back and it was blown up. Now I'm not being able to switch it back on again!'

Now there's a surprise, I thought.

I pointed out that painting the glass valves of his black and white TV would not render it coloured and that if he decided to try anything else like this again he should think twice, and go to D. E. R. Rentals and hire one instead. 'That way, my dear friend, there would be less chance of blowing yourself up, along with the entire street of tenement buildings in Govanhill. But more importantly, it will prevent you from making a surprise and unexpected touchdown back home in Istanbul!'

Haemorrhoid Man

• • •

Unfortunately, I bumped into you know who again. That's twice within a week; I can only hope that my luck will get better.

Having worked on the same shift as him, I was responsible for labelling him with the nickname 'The Itch', because he got under not only my skin, but everybody who knew him.

'I'm going in for an operation!' he greeted me.

'Nothing trivial I hope!' I responded bluntly, but it was out before I could stop myself.

'I can't close my hands shut,' he said, demonstrating.

'That'll be a change for you then; we could never get you to open them. Particularly when it was your turn to pay for a round of drinks!' I responded abruptly.

'Are you still writing those books about us all?' he asked.

'Why not? It gives my readers a good laugh!' I said.

'I've got three of them, but I never bought them,' he emphasised. 'It was the wife that got me them,' he said. 'They're a load of shite; I wouldn't waste my money!'

'Well, at least one half of your family has taste,' I responded.

'Am I in your latest book then?' he asked eagerly.

'Ah Cannae Tell a Lie! But definitely. I could write an entire series of books about you alone. You're so full of shite, it just flows out of every orifice,' I replied sarcastically.

'Do you really mean that, Harry?' he asked sincerely.

'No!' I responded immediately. 'I'm lying, But if I should ever write about you, I'll refer to you as "Haemorrhoid Man".'

'Haemorrhoid Man?' he asked.

'Exactly! You were a complete and total pain in the arse, and by all accounts – having been unfortunate enough to bump into you twice within a week – nothing has changed!'

Y'know, sometimes it does you good to get it off your chest!

The Village Bobby

• • •

It was PC Henderson's last day on the beat after thirty years police service, all of which he had loyally served in the village of Lochwinnoch.

When he arrived on his beat that morning, he was greeted by the local councillor and his family, who all hugged and congratulated him and presented him with a cheque for £100.

Further along the road, he entered the church, where the pastor presented him with an 18-carat gold fob watch on behalf of the congregation.

As he left the church he was met by the members of the local Probus club, who gave him a bottle of fine malt whisky.

PC Henderson was smiling from ear to ear when he left them and had only walked a few hundred metres along the road, when he heard a female voice beckoning him from a nearby window.

He approached the house, where he was met at the door by a dumb blonde in her negligee.

She reached out and, taking him by the arm, she led him up the stairs to the bedroom, where they made the most passionate love he had ever experienced, after which, when it was all over, they went downstairs and she cooked him a full breakfast of bacon, eggs, sausage and potato scone, with fresh orange juice.

As she was pouring him a cup of coffee, PC Henderson noticed a £10 note sticking out from under the cup.

'This day has just been too wonderful for words,' he said, 'but can I ask what the ten-pound note is for?'

'Well, I must admit, that was my husband's idea!' replied the blonde. 'Last night, when I was telling him that today would be your last day on the village beat and that we should do something special for you, he said, "Fuck him. Give him a tenner!' She then gave him a cute smile and, winking her eye, said, 'By the way, the breakfast was my idea!'

Fact or Fiction?

• • •

Hi there, this is a wee note to the young guy who approached me the other night, pulled out a rather large knife and demanded that I hand over my black North Face jacket and wallet.

Remember me?

You also asked my missus for her purse and jewellery.

I really hope you somehow come across this message, for I really feel I should apologise for my out of character actions.

I didn't expect you to react so badly, as I genuinely thought you looked like a tough guy, committing this act on your own, but you burst into tears and physically shat your trousers when, while busily trying on my jacket, you looked up and saw me pointing my .44 Magnum handgun at you.

The truth is, I was wearing my jacket for a reason that night, and it wasn't to keep me warm, but you know that now.

As it was, you were identified for mugging my sister the previous night and as I just happened to receive my Magnum replica pistol from an American friend for Christmas, along with a shoulder holster, I decided to try it on that evening, while out walking in your area, praying we would bump into each other.

As luck would have it, the power of prayer worked and, well, the rest as we say is history! Beautiful gun, don't you think?

'A very intimidating weapon,' stated the advert. Well I

don't need to tell you that; you already know first hand . . . Am I right?

I'll bet you didn't enjoy the long walk home, back to wherever you'd crawled out from, with all that smelly brown stuff flopping about in your fancy new tracksuit trousers.

I'm sure it was made all the worse with me insisting that you leave your new Nike training shoes, Sony Ericsson mobile phone that plays 'Gangsta's Paradise' as a ring tone, and your black Gucci leather wallet with me.

There was no way I was going to let you use it to call up your buddies to come and help you try to mug the mugger you were mugging. Pretty ironic, son, eh?

By the way, I knew you wouldn't mind, so I took the liberty of calling your mother, or 'Mammy', as you had her listed in your phone, and explaining to her your predicament at that time and to run you a hot bubble bath.

I also bought my sister and my missus the biggest bouquets of flowers and I of course used your Visa credit card to pay for them. My sister thought that was a really nice gesture by you!

Your Nike trainers were too small for me, so I gave them to one of the homeless guys selling the Big Issue outside my local supermarket, and the cash left in your wallet went to the Cancer Research charity shop.

Honestly, you would have been so proud of me – sorry, you!

Unfortunately, I have to admit that I couldn't resist using your mobile to call several of those phone sex numbers, you know the ones. They charge an arm and a leg per minute, but I have no doubt you'll see that for yourself when you get your phone bill in from Vodafone. Better you than me.

Mind you, they did cut me off after the third day, just when I was about to make some threatening calls to the Procurator Fiscal's office on your behalf!

Anyways, with regards to your fancy tracksuit trousers. The missus thinks I was a bit over the top with the summary justice I meted out to you, because technically, you didn't really mug us; 'we mugged you!

So, I'd like to make it up to you by apologising for making you walk all the way back home with no shoes on your feet and covered in your own excrement, however, the alternative would have been to shoot you!

I'm genuinely hoping that you'll reconsider the path you have chosen in life. I shouldn't say it, but I enjoyed the role reversal.

However, the next time you might not get someone as forgiving and easygoing as me – and the missus, of course!

By the way, if you go on to be a real gangster and write a book glamourising all the crimes you committed, mind and dedicate a chapter to the night we met. I would love to read your version of events!

The Facecloth

· · ·

I had been working with a younger policeman who, during a refreshment break in our shift, confided in me over a cup of coffee that he was suffering from painful, bleeding piles.

He told me he had finally overcome the embarrassment to arrange for a haemorrhoid examination with his GP later in the week.

Early one morning, two days prior to his appointment, he received a call from his doctor's office to tell him that due to a cancellation, he had been rescheduled for that morning at nine thirty.

He hadn't been in bed long, having just worked a twelve-hour nightshift duty, and it was already around eight forty-five a.m.

Knowing the trip to his GP's office would take about twenty-five minutes, he didn't have too much time to spare.

Like most men, he liked to take a little extra effort over his hygiene, particularly when making such visits, but this time he wasn't going to be able to make the full effort.

He rushed to the bathroom, threw off his pyjamas, wet the facecloth that was sitting next to the sink, and gave himself a quick wash in that area to make sure he was at least presentable.

He threw the facecloth into the washing basket, quickly got dressed, jumped into his car, and raced off to make his appointment.

He was in the waiting room for only a few minutes when his name was called.

Having had a similar complaint several years ago, I had made him aware of what would happen during such an examination.

Knowing what to expect, he confidently walked straight in, dropped his trousers and pants, hopped up onto the table, looked over at the other side of the room and pretended to be anywhere else in the country other than lying in a GP's surgery with his bare buttocks blatantly exposed to another man, doctor or not!

However, he was a little surprised when the doctor remarked, 'My oh my, Mr Kerr, we have made an extra effort this morning, haven't we?'

Being in such an uncompromising position, he didn't pay too much attention to this comment, or even consider responding.

After the examination, he heaved a huge sigh of relief, left the surgery and went home.

The rest of his day was normal – a few hours' sleep, followed by some lunch, before his children returned home from school.

Later that afternoon, while his six-year-old daughter was playing, she called out from the bathroom, 'Mummy, where's my facecloth?'

His wife responded by telling her to get another one from the cupboard.

His young daughter became very upset and called out, 'No, Mummy! I need the one that was here next to the sink; it has all my sparkly glitter saved up inside it!'

To this day, the facecloth has never been found and he's never told his wife about it either, or how the bed just happened to be covered in glitter.

Oh, and suffice to say, he has never gone back to the doctor for his results.

But apparently his wife thinks the sun shines out of his arse anyway!

I Left It There!

· · ·

John Garvan was one of those young cops who was an instant favourite with the supervisors, particularly the shift inspector who noticeably detailed him 'good duties' and put him ahead of other waiting cops to sit his police driving test.

Having passed the test with flying colours, John superseded more senior cops by being given one of the regular Panda cars to patrol in, while they continued to walk a beat.

One night shift, John recovered an abandoned stolen car.

After he completed the relevant checks on the stolen vehicle, the radio controller instructed him to remain with the car, as the owner had been contacted and was coming to collect it.

While waiting for the owner to appear, a call was broadcast regarding housebreakers at a shop several miles away.

The beat officers, along with the divisional crime car, responded to the call, attending from nearby.

John decided to respond to the call also, but was instructed by the controller to remain where he was, standing by the stolen car

Moments later, fed up waiting for the car owner to arrive, and without notifying the controller of his intentions, John drove off in his Panda to assist with the housebreakers.

By the time he arrived at the shop, those in attendance had already apprehended the housebreakers and were about to convey them to the police station.

John walked about chatting with those he knew, when he was interrupted by the controller, requesting his position for the car owner, who had arrived to collect his car, only to find it missing.

It turned out that after John left his position by the stolen car, the car thief returned and promptly stole it again!

Reprimanded for his neglect of duty, John lost his Panda car and was destined to walk the beat for a very long time. He eventually had enough of it and resigned from the police!

The Care Worker

...

My old colleague Martin Barrett made a rare visit to my house the other night and we sat down for a wee blether over a bottle of my favourite tipple.

Martin is in his late sixties, but apart from his white mop of hair and pale complexion, he looks much younger than his age. I'm only saying that just in case he reads this. You know how vain some guys are?

During our conversation, I was enquiring about his elderly mother, who was showing signs of senile dementia.

'Well fortunately I've managed to secure the help of the local healthcare for the area, where carers call in the morning to assist her out of bed, dress her and make her breakfast before leaving. They come back at lunchtime to check on her, and make her lunch. Then at teatime, they pay her another visit and give her some soup or scrambled egg to tide her over till the following morning.

'Finally, a nightshift carer arrives to help her into her pyjamas and see her safely into bed, before switching off all the lights and locking up the house.'

'What an excellent service that is,' I said. 'You must be really pleased with that.'

'I suppose so, but they do get some things wrong now and again, and you wonder if they know what they're doing,' he replied.

'Like what?' I asked, eager to know.

'Well just the other morning, having visited my mother over the weekend, I decided to stay on until Monday before I travelled back down south. Anyway, I drank a large whisky before going off to bed, and fell into a deep sleep. Suddenly, I was aroused by the bedroom door opening and a female appeared at the side of my bed, touching my arm. I thought it was a dream, as she rubbed it gently to waken me up and said, "Wakey, wakey, Mister Barrett, would you like me to help you into the toilet and then give you a wee wash down?"

'I was startled, as I looked up at her leaning over me, while I focussed my sleepy eyes on her and said, "It's not me you're here to help, it's my mother in the next room!"'

Thirty Days

. . .

George Ewart was the police sergeant on the *Semper Vigilo* boat, but he was also heavily involved in amateur boxing with the Scotland team, where he helped train and referee fights.

He told me of one incident where the team were all to meet up, to be transported to a boxing contest in Manchester.

George noticed that two of our best medal hopes were missing from the group and made enquiries as to their whereabouts. He was informed that one of them had been involved in an alleged assault and breach of the peace.

Moments later, as everyone was boarding the bus to leave, one of the boxers turned up at the last minute.

George asked him what had happened to the other, missing boxer, and he cheekily replied in a rhyme, 'Thirty days has September, April, June and Henry Albert!'

Mutual Advice

· · ·

Donnie Henderson's son is a chip off the old block. I'm told he was sitting on a bench in the shopping mall, munching away on one chocolate bar after another.

While chewing his way through a fourth, a man sitting opposite him said, 'Hey, wee man, did ye know eating aw they chocolate bars isnae good for ye? It'll gie ye plooks, rot yer teeth, and make you fat.'

Donnie Junior replied, 'My granda lived to be ninety-four years auld.'

The man said, 'That might be true, son, but did yer granda eat four chocolate bars, one after another?'

Donnie Junior replied, 'Naw, he just minded his ain bloody business!'

Picking up the Pieces

· · ·

It was the start to a weekend and I was partnered with auld Bob MacDonald. An experienced cop of senior years, he had seen it all, bought the tee shirt, etc, etc.

We had only just left the office when we received our first call to attend a large street fight, involving several males, outside the subway at Govan Cross.

Eager to get there, I had to be restrained by Bob, who insisted in setting a snail's pace.

On our arrival at the scene, the males were unaware of our presence, as Bob led me into a nearby tenement close to take observations and view the proceedings from a safe distance.

He then explained to me that we would enter the fracas at the finish, when they had all but punched themselves out.

Sure enough, as they tired themselves out, we stepped out from the tenement and made our presence known to them, and on seeing us in full uniform, most of them hobbled, staggered and limped off, apart from two of them, who feigned unconsciousness and remained lying on the roadway.

Auld Bob casually walked over and gave them both a kick, but true to their tremendous acting skills, they lay impassively still.

At that, Bob bent down and tied both their working boot laces together in a knot, and called for the police van to attend.

Several moments later, the police van could be heard

nearing the location, and as a result, both men got to their feet and tried to run off, but very quickly fell flat on their faces.

Due to the wisdom and experience of Auld Bob, it turned out to be an easy apprehension of two previously violent males.

However, Bob did point out to me that even if they had got out of their tied boots, a shipyard docker would never leave his working boots behind him, as he would miss out on the overtime on the Sunday if he had no boots to wear.

The auld polis experience and technique at its ultimate best here, and long before computer technology.

Whatever happened to the use of simple common sense?

Deathbed Confession

· · ·

Glasgow's gangster underworld was recently mourning the death of one of its oldest, respected rivals.

However, the word on the street is that he died from something completely different from what was first announced.

It appears that during a long, drawn-out illness, he was nearing death's door, and called on his wife to be near him.

'Pat! Pat! I need you to listen to my last confession. I need to tell you something before I die,' he said.

His wife took his hand and caressed it gently. 'Don't be silly, darling. You've never confessed to anything in your entire life, and I don't want to hear you doing so now!' she replied.

'But Pat!' he said, grabbing hold of her arm. 'I need to tell you, so that I can be forgiven and have a clear conscience!'

'It's not necessary, darling. Save your breath. Just forget it.'

'I can't forget it, and I can't go from this world without getting it off my chest,' he replied.

'There is absolutely no need for you to confess anything! You've never done it in the past, so why start now?' Pat said.

'Pat! Will you bloody listen to me? I'm trying to break it gently, but there's no other way to tell you, hen . . . I slept with your young sister! And I've slept with your best pal, Tracy! I nearly slept with your brother! But worse than that, darling, I've even slept with your mammy! What do you have to say about that?'

Pat hesitated for a moment, giving the impression she was deeply shocked by this despicable confession, before bending down and whispering happily into his ear, 'I know all about it! And that's why I poisoned you, you bastard!'

The Man Who Would Be King!

• • •

Fed up hearing about how the other cops on his shift are treated like kings in their own house, John went to his local library and found a book entitled *Be the King of Your Castle*.

After several days of intense reading, he strode into the marital home and boldly announced to his estranged wife, 'From this moment on, you need to know that I am the king of this house and what I say is law.

'You, my dear wife, will pour me a glass of the finest Chateauneuf du Pape tonight, which I will sit back and savour, while you prepare for me a gourmet dinner, and when I'm finished eating it, you will then serve me up a delicious chocolate dessert followed by coffee and mints.

'After that, you will follow me upstairs and we will indulge in the kind of insatiable sex that I desire.

'Then, and only then, when I am sufficiently satisfied, you will run me a hot Radox bath so that I can totally relax in the comfort of the bubbles, illuminated by scented candles, during which time you will shampoo my hair, sponge my chest and back and towel me dry before helping me on with my towelling bath robe.

'We will then return to the bedroom, where you will gently massage my feet and hands with aromatherapy oils until I fall asleep.

'Then, tomorrow morning, take a guess who is going to wash and shave me, dress me in my best double-breasted suit and brush my hair?'

His wife stood up, looked him straight in the eye and replied, 'The fucking funeral director would be my first guess!'

Deep Shit!

. . .

A call went out that there were horses wandering about the roadway in Newton, after straying from a nearby farmer's field.

One mobile station went to the locus of the stray horses to round them up, while Donnie in the other police Panda went to the farm to inform the farmer to attend.

As he drove along the lengthy driveway to the farmhouse, his attention was drawn to the farmer waving his arms vigorously from the front of the farm yard.

Thinking that there was another incident taking place, Donnie accelerated faster towards him, only to be confronted by a rather irate farmer, who announced, 'You've just driven your bloody car along my newly laid driveway, which I've only just finished concreting!'

Medicine Man

• • •

During a routine visit to the police station by the police casualty surgeon, to examine a prisoner, the duty officer Inspector 'Captain' Wright took advantage of his presence to obtain some advice and describe his own symptoms.

The police casualty surgeon recommended that he should take some medication for his condition and handed him a couple of tablets, which he promptly swallowed down.

A few moments later, having submitted his medical report, the police surgeon was preparing to leave when Captain Wright enquired about the health of the prisoner and asked if he required any medication.

To which the police surgeon replied, 'Yes! I gave you two very strong sleeping tablets for him! Night! Night! Captain Wright!'

Glesca, God's Country

. . .

One day during my 'Harry the Polis' tour about the UK, I was in Manchester.

I entered a church, the interior of which was so beautiful that I decided to take some photographs.

Whilst doing so, I spotted a golden telephone mounted on the wall with a sign above it that read: '£1,000 per call.'

I was very intrigued by this and asked a priest who was strolling by what the golden telephone was used for.

The priest replied that it was a direct line to heaven and that for £1,000 you could talk personally to God.

I thanked the priest and went on my way.

My next stop was in the Blue Room, Liverpool.

The following day, after my show, I visited a very large cathedral, where I saw the same golden telephone with a replica sign above it.

I wondered if this was the same kind of telephone I had seen in Manchester and asked the minister what its purpose was.

He explained to me that it was a direct line to heaven and for only £1,000 I could speak directly to God.

I thanked him very much, made my excuses and left.

I then travelled to Southport, Bolton, Blackburn, Leeds and Newcastle.

In every church I visited, I saw the same golden telephone with the same '£1,000 per call' sign above it.

On my arrival back home in Scotland, I decided to visit Glasgow Cathedral to see if they had the same telephone.

I entered the cathedral and looked around, and sure

enough, there was the same golden telephone, but this time the sign above it read: '£1.00 per call.'

I was somewhat surprised by this, so I spoke with the Chaplain, Mister Morris, about the sign.

'Sir, I've travelled all over the UK and I've seen this same golden telephone in many churches. I'm told that it is a direct line to heaven, where the caller can speak personally with God, but in England the price was £1,000 per call. How come it is so cheap here?' I asked.

The chaplain smiled and replied, 'You're back home in Scotland, Harry, it's just a local call from here.'

Fire in the Hole

• • •

One day, an ex-army hand grenade was handed into divisional headquarters by a relative of a deceased person, who discovered it while helping to clear the house.

The grenade was taken to the CID office and put into the 'Bomb Box', a sand-filled metal cylinder, which was then taken into the basement of the police office, and the Bomb Squad in Edinburgh were duly informed to attend.

Detective Inspector Fabian, who was present when it was handed in, assumed command of the situation.

However, unbeknown to everyone in the police station, he went downstairs to the basement, removed the suspect grenade from the Bomb Box and carried it along to his office, where he played with it for a short while before pulling out the firing pin and rolling it down the long corridor towards the typing pool and senior officers' department. He then followed up this action by loudly shouting, 'Fire in the hole!'

Fortunately for DI Fabian and the office staff on that floor, the suspect grenade did not explode.

However, on the arrival and subsequent examination by the Bomb Squad, they immediately evacuated the building when it was discovered that the grenade was live and that only its rusted condition had prevented it from exploding.

The Bomb Squad then carried out a controlled explosion within nearby Glasgow Green.

As for DI Fabian, he retired under a Section 8 assessment carried out by the Chief Medical Officer.

Itchy Powder

• • •

At one time, many years ago, the local council would set aside a number of houses within an area, specifically for serving police officers and their families.

One particular night, a call was received regarding a domestic disturbance at the police housing area.

A police van from 'A' Division was dispatched to deal with the incident.

On their arrival, they saw an off-duty cop, still in uniform, involved in a punch-up with his wife.

The attending cops intervened and tried to ascertain what the problem was, during which both wanted to make counter charges.

It appeared that the wife had developed a rather itchy red rash, downstairs in her private region, and was curious to know where it had come from.

Surprise, surprise! The cop also confessed to having a similar itchy red rash in his private region.

The cop also freely admitted that drinking was his vice, not sleeping around, and therefore, as far as he was concerned, it must have been his wife who had been playing around.

Fortunately, the senior cop in attendance at the call was a mature married policewoman, who used her common sense and asked the itchy wife how she went about doing the family washing.

'I always separate my pants and his drawers, and soak them first, before washing them. As you'll know, men always stink!' she said.

She then produced the powder shc used, which was a new brand of biological washing powder.

'I always put a bit extra powder in to make sure it removes his noticeable skid marks!' she added.

'That's it! That's your problem,' replied the police-woman.

She then proceeded to explain that it was possibly the toxic chemicals in the washing powder that were causing an allergic reaction with their privates, after coming into contact with the pants. The policewoman then offered a guaranteed solution to the itchy woman's problems.

'Gie yer drawers an extra and more thorough rinse through next time!'

Her final piece of advice was for them to make up, apply some soothing Sudocrem to their itchy areas, and for an added little 'spice' to their night, she suggested that they both go around 'commando' and refrain from wearing any underwear for the next few days.

The couple left the house, with the convinced wife now seeking out the soothing cream required to apply on her exonerated husband's itchy bits.

Problem solved and love was in the air once again.

But another explanation that came my way was that during this itchy rash period, several cops on his shift had also experienced a similar irritating itch to their privates.

Apparently, several of his patrol shift had represented the division, along with himself, at a police football match.

During the game, whilst everyone was out on the football park, a certain PC Alex Craig from 'A' Division arrived at the game via a slight detour, having made a fleeting visit to Tam Sheppard's joke shop.

On his arrival, he entered the vacant dressing rooms, and lightly sprinkled some fast-action itching powder into the opposing divisional team's discarded underwear.

Now that would appear to me to be more like the real truth!

Although sometimes, due to their drink problems, several of my colleagues in 'F' Division have to get down on their knees and thank the guys in 'A' Division for providing them, and their lovely wives, with a very full and satisfying sex life.

Allegedly!

Get the Point

· · ·

Big Bob, a serving police officer from Glasgow, had been a regular visitor to Crete, Greece, for many years, and had befriended most of the local police.

One day, he was drinking with an elderly on-duty cop in a local pub, situated at the corner of a very busy road junction, which the old cop was meant to be supervising.

Being a few weeks away from his official retirement from the police, the old cop had been transferred there, as his final posting, more or less to keep him out of trouble.

However, being well known and popular with the locals, everyone was plying him with free booze.

The junction suddenly became gridlocked with the lunchtime traffic and due to the fact that the old cop was now completely rat-arsed, he handed Bob his hat, jacket and whistle and beckoned for him to take control of the junction.

Being an ex-city centre cop, big Bob took it in his stride and performed the duty of points man admirably, so much so that a local wrote a letter of commendation to the chief of police about the traffic control and how the police officer who performed this duty regularly looked so much younger after his obvious loss of weight and removal of his trademark moustache!

The old cop was so proud of his written commendation that he showed everybody in the pub the letter, which was in Greek, and signed by the chief of police.

He then invited Bob to come to the pub every day during his family holiday and take charge of the busy junction, should he ever get so pissed again.

As for the local who wrote in the letter of commendation, he turned out to be one of the regulars who were in the pub that day drinking alongside them!

Last Request

· · ·

Three highly decorated police officers were killed at a shoot-out during a raid on some drug dealer's home, and all arrived in heaven at the same time.

St Peter greeted all three officers at the pearly gates and asked, 'In a few days' time, when you are laid out to rest in your casket, and your fellow officers and your loving families are mourning over you, what words would you like to hear them say about you?'

The first cop said, 'I would like to hear them say that I was a good father, and one of the bravest cops in the squad!'

The second police officer said, 'I would like to hear them say that I was a great cop to work with and one who bravely died in the line of duty.'

The last cop paused for a moment, then replied, 'More than anything, I would like to hear them shouting out loudly, "Look! He's moving!"'

Spice of Life

. . .

There were three women friends, all working in the same office. One was involved in a casual relationship with a police inspector, one was engaged to be married to a police sergeant, and the third was the long-time wife of a Govan beat cop. They got together for drinks after work one day. The conversation eventually drifted towards how best to spice up their sex lives.

After much discussion, they decided to surprise their men by each engaging in some S&M role playing for them.

The following week, all three women met up to compare notes on how they had got on.

Sipping on her drink, the single girl leered and said, 'Last Friday, at the end of our work, I went to my boyfriend's station wearing a long leather coat. When no-one else was about and we were alone in his office, I locked the door, slipped out of my coat and all I had on was a leather bodice, black net stockings and stiletto heels.

He was so aroused that we made mad, passionate love on top of his desk, right then and there!'

The engaged woman giggled and said, 'That's pretty much the same as my story! When my fiancé came home last Friday, I was waiting for him in a black mask, leather bodice, black hose and stiletto pumps.

He was so turned on that we not only made love the entire night, but he wants to bring our wedding date forward!'

The married woman put her glass down and said, 'I put

a lot of thought into it, and I did a lot of planning. I made arrangements for the kids to stay overnight at Grandma's.

'I took a long scented-oil bath and then put on my best perfume before slipping into a tight leather bodice, a black garter belt, black fishnet stockings and six-inch stilettos.

'I finished it off with a black mask, ready for action.

'My husband arrived home from work, took one look at me standing there, grabbed a beer from the fridge, picked up the remote control, sat his arse down in front of the TV and yelled out, "Hey Batman! What's for my dinner?"'

Old Aged Polis

. . .

Two elderly retired polis were sitting on a park bench, under a tree one day. One turned to the other and said, 'You know, Sam, I'm eighty-two years old and I'm just full of aches and pains. Now you're about the same age. How do you feel?'

Sam replied, 'I feel like a newborn baby!'

'Really! Like a newborn baby?' he asked.

'Yeah! I've no hair, no teeth, and I think I've just shit my pants!'

All About Ivy

. . .

This is a nice little Bible story about Eve and the Garden of Eden, loosely interpreted and given a modern day Glesca slant.

After almost three weeks in the Botanic Gardens, the big man paid wee Ivy a flying visit, to check on her progress.

'So, Ivy, how's it gaun, hen?' he enquired.

'It's gaun really well, boss, and efter a wee brush and polish, the place is looking no' too bad,' she replied. 'Ah mean, even the sunrises and sunsets are absolutely breathtaking, and the scented aromas, what can Ah say? The smells and the sights are just fan-dabi-dozi.'

'Aw, that's great, hen, I'm glad ye're settling in!' God said.

'Well, I am and I umnac!' she responded.

God was taken by surprise by this remark from Ivy. 'Whit is it, hen? Whit's getting up yer humph noo? Tell me.'

'Well, it's no' a big thing, boss, but it's these breasts you've bunged me with. The one in the middle is pushing the other two out the bed, so tae speak, and I'm forever banging them wi' my arms. They just seem tae catch on aw the branches in the garden, and they keep getting snagged on bushes. Particularly they jaggy brambles. They're becoming a real pain in the—'

God interrupted before she could finish the sentence. 'I think I get the message, Ivy, no need to blaspheme!'

After a short while in her company, Ivy went on to tell God that since many other parts of her body were made up of pairs, such as her legs, arms, eyes, ears, and so on, she felt that by having just the two breasts, it might make her body more symmetrically balanced, better looking, and less of an oddity, as she put it.

'That's a fair point you make, hen,' replied God, rubbing his chin. 'But you've got to remember, it was my first attempt at this, you know. I mean, Ah gave aw the animals six breasts, so I figured that as a wummin, you would use only half of them, but I suppose looking at ye noo, Ah can see that you are right. Leave it with me and I'll figure oot somethin' else.'

Several moments went by, then God yelled out, 'Got it!'

He reached over, removed the middle breast from Ivy and tossed it over his shoulder, into the nearby bushes.

'There ye go, hen. Problem solved and, if I say so myself, ye look so much better already!'

With this small miracle completed, God bade Ivy a fond farewell and left to check on the rest of his creations.

Two weeks later, while God was going around checking on his kingdom, he decided once again to pop in for a flying visit and a wee spiritual cup o' tea with Ivy at the Botanic Gardens.

'Hello Ivy hen. How's my favourite creation today?'

'Ah'm just fantastic, boss!' she replied. 'However, there's just one wee oversight on your part. Nothing big, mind you.'

God interrupted her, 'Ye want a dishwasher?'

'Naw Ah don't want a dishwasher!' she replied.

'Ah know! Ye want a Hoover? I'll get ye a Dyson,' he said.

'Naw! Ah don't want a dishwasher and Ah don't need a Dyson . . . yet!'

'Well, whit is it then?' asked God, eager to please her.

'Right! It's like this. Every other creature in the garden appears tae have a partner. For example, the animals are paired off, the ewe has a ram and the cow has her bull. Crikey! Even wee Jimmy Krankie has a mate. Everybody! Except for me.

'Ah don't mind telling ye, boss, I've naebody tae talk with and I'm beginning tae feel very lonely in here masel'.'

God digested everything Ivy had said to him, and over a cup of tea and a Tunnocks caramel wafer, he thought about her request to have a partner for several moments, before speaking.

'You know, Ivy hen, Ah think ye're right. How could I have been so blind as to overlook this? Ye dae need a mate and Ah'm gonnae get straight tae work immediately and create for you a proper partner from a part of you.

'Now let me see . . . where did I toss that useless tit?'

Now does that not sound much more believable than all that other stuff about a rib?

Drunk Aye, Daft Naw!

· · ·

Along with John Riley, I had just taken up duty and was leaving Craigie Street police office when we came across a drunk male, sitting in the lane at the rear of the office.

As we stopped to talk with him, it was obvious he was incapable of taking care of himself, so for his own safety, we picked him up and led him in the back door of the office.

During a search of his person, we discovered he had trousers on under his working boiler suit, and in the pockets, we found £1,720 in £10 notes, all rolled tightly together. So in effect, we had done him a favour by lifting him and prevented the prospect of him being relieved of his money by some opportunist.

The male was taken into custody and put into a cell to sleep it off while John and I continued with our duties.

Several hours later, in the early hours of the morning, the duty officer was making a check of his prisoners, in order to see who could be released from custody.

When he approached the cell of the drunk male, he called him and wakened him up. Once awake, he then asked him how much he'd had to drink.

'Aboot fifteen or sixteen pints,' replied the male.

The duty officer then asked him, 'On a scale of one to ten, one being completely sober and ten being totally drunk, where would you say that you are?'

'Ah might be drunk, son, but Ah'm no' daft.'

'No-one is suggesting that, but where would you say you are then?' he asked again.

Quick as a flash he replied, 'That's easy, Craigie Street! I think!'

Serenity or Senility?

· · ·

I was attending a funeral service along with my mother. It turned out to be the husband of one of ladies from her church.

After the ceremony, everyone was invited back to the church hall for tea and sandwiches.

While standing beside the very elderly widow, my mother was talking to her and asked, 'So how old was your husband?'

'He was ninety-four!' she replied. 'Two years older than me.'

'Ninety-four? So that makes you . . . ninety-two?' she said.

'That's correct. I'm ninety-two years old!' she replied proudly.

My mother paused for a moment, before responding. 'It's hardly worth your while going home, hen, is it?'

The Court Case

...

This is an actual Australian Court docket #12659, 'The case of the pregnant lady.'

The case refers to a lady about nine months pregnant who was travelling as a passenger on a bus. During her journey, she noticed the young man opposite was smiling at her. She immediately changed her position and moved to another seat. However, this time his smile turned to a grin, making her feel uneasy and prompting her to move once again.

The young man appeared even more amused by this. Moving for a fourth time, the man burst into uncontrollable laughter.

As a result of this, the woman complained to the driver, who contacted the police, and the young man was arrested.

The case was called at court, during which the judge asked the young man what he had to say for himself.

The young man replied, 'Well, your honour, it was like this. I was already a passenger on the bus when this lady got on, and I couldn't help notice her obvious condition. So when she sat down on her seat opposite me, under a sign that read, "The Double Mint Twins Are Coming", I couldn't help but grin.

'Then the lady got up and changed seats and sat under another sign that read, "Logan's Liniment Reduces Swelling", I just had to smile at that.

'She then got up from her seat and moved again, sitting under a deodorant sign that read, "William's Big Stick Did

The Trick", by which point I could hardly contain myself. But your honour, when she moved for a fourth time and sat under a sign that read, "Goodyear Rubber Could Have Prevented This Accident", I'm afraid, I just lost it!'

Result of the court: CASE DISMISSED!

Fitness Club

• • •

Having been retired from the police for several years now, I felt that my old 'Jean Brody' was getting a bit out of shape, so with my wife's permission, I joined a local fitness club and started my exercise regime.

First I went to the aerobics class for seniors.

I bent over, twisted my hips, gyrated like a young John Travolta, jogged on the spot, and sweated that much I thought I had Oxo cubes under my armpits.

By the time I got my tracksuit on, the bloody class was over!

Whyte & MacKay Health Drink

· · ·

To all my friends who enjoy a wee glass of wine . . . And those who enjoy a cheeky wee glass of H_2O.

As Ben Franklin once said: 'In wine there is wisdom, in beer there is freedom, and in water there is bacteria.' And by all accounts, there would appear to be a lot of it!

In a number of carefully controlled trials, scientists have discovered through tests that if we drink one litre of water each day, by the end of the year we will have personally absorbed more than one kilo of Escherichia coli, better known as E. Coli, the deadly bacteria found in faeces.

In other words, we are consuming one kilo of poop per annum.

However, apparently we do NOT run the same risk when drinking wine, beer, tequila, rum, whisky or any other liquor, because alcohol has to go through a purification process of boiling, filtering and fermenting.

Remember what they're saying here. Water equals 'Poo'. And we're not talking friendly old 'Winnie the Pooh' here.

And alcohol equals 'Health'!

Which is something that I have been personally advocating to friends and colleagues for many a year.

Therefore, it would appear to be slightly more costly, but extremely more beneficial to our health, to drink alcohol and talk absolute and utter pish, than consume pints of inexpensive clear tap water and be full of shit.

There is no need to thank me for bringing this valuable information to your attention, because it was one of my ex-colleagues who came across the article and considered it as his public duty to forward it on to me to highlight it, knowing that I was always in the shit as a cop!

So I'm basically doing this as a public service for my fellow human beings.

In saying that, if anyone out there would like to nominate me for a mention in the New Year Honours List, or even just a presentation bottle of whisky from my favourite duo, Whyte & Mackay, then by all means go for it! Cheers.

Wee Jock is Back!

• • •

Those who read my books will be well aware of wee Jock, my trusted four-legged friend who last appeared in *Even More Lies*.

Although a Yorkshire Terrier, he does tend to think he's a Rottweiler. God only knows what mirror he's looking in.

He went out for a walk the other day and when he arrived back he was totally wasted – and I don't mean drunk; I mean the blushing, embarrassed sort of wasted.

'Where have you been? I was whistling for you for ages. The neighbours must have thought that Roger Whittaker was performing an open-air concert in the car park!' I said.

'Well you should have shouted me, I'm no deaf!' he replied.

'So you did hear me then?' I asked.

'Aye, Ah heard ye, but I was busy with a burd!'

'A bird? I take it you mean a bitch?' I said. 'Are you hanging about outside the door of some bitch on heat, boy?

If you are, you'll end up with somebody sticking their big Doc Marten boot right up your arse.'

'Naw! Naw! It's nothing like that. It's yon big good-looking blonde polis woman. She's got the hots for me. Ah saw her staunin' in the bus shelter. She was doing a school crossing, so Ah just sidled up beside her, had a quick look up her dress before rubbing myself against her leg and cocking my head to one side to give her my cute look. You know the one!' he replied.

'Did she no' wallop you with her baton?' I asked.

'Not at all, she picked me up, gave me a cuddle and pushed my face between her big bazookas and then tried tae sook the face aff me. She's a big lassie, that yin, wi' a cracking pair o' tits!'

'Well it wouldn't be me. I'd have booted you in the balls if I'd seen you doing that, ya dirty wee perv! If she comes to this door and complains about you, you're going to the vet for—'

He interrupted me. 'Hawd yer horses there, Harry. She loved it. She thinks I'm right cuddly and cute – just like that Kate Adie, remember I told you about her, the time when I was helping out at the Iranian Embassy siege? See, the likes of me, I can get away with that, 'cause I'm wee. Ah just put my head tae the side and the women are all over me like a rash, wanting tae cuddle me, kiss me, feed me sweeties and rub my belly.

'Now, if you tried it, well that's a different story! You'd definitely get kicked in the R.S. McColls,' Jock explained.

'So how is it different for a manky wee bugger like you to do it?' I asked, looking for an explanation.

'Because, as I've already explained, I'm cute and cuddly, that's why women melt when they see me. Hence the reason when Ah rub myself against them, or give them a French kiss while licking their face, they take it as a bit of affection from man's best friend, 'cause I'm just a wee friendly dug that they all love!'

'I must remember to add that description to your Kennel Club pedigree. It might make you worth more when I sell you! So how long have you been doing this wee act?'

'Tut! Tut! Is that a bit of jealousy creeping into your vocabulary and finding its way out of your big mouth?'

'Definitely not! But I certainly don't want people stopping me in the street and complaining about you trying to indecently interfere with their leg,' I said, trying to make a point.

'Look, Jock, you're a wee dog. Have you never been with another canine of your own breed since I got you? I mean to say, your no' exactly Rin Tin Tin in the looks department, but you're better looking than that big Floyd up the next close. So, tell me. When was the last time?'

'Yesterday!' he responded immediately. 'A wee Lhassa Apso called Sally from Giffnock! She ran away from her owner in the Rouken Glen Park and wandered up here looking for a bit of rough on the side and I just happened to be out for a walk on my own and clocked her.'

'I hope you took precautions and had protected sex?' I said.

'Of course I did. We did it in a bus shelter. Much better than a street corner, don't you think? Anyways, I didnae want any of they mongrels about here seeing her and getting a bad name; she's fae a good family. Her mother and father were both champions and her granny won a first at Crufts.'

'I'm pleased to hear that you only have it off with the best of breeds, none of your Heinz 57 variety!' I remarked.

'Look, Harry! Ah cannae stop a grown woman if she wants tae pick me up tae cuddle me, it's in my nature tae be nice. And Ah love the attention they give me,' he said.

'But you shouldn't let them pick you up like that!' I responded. 'Makes you look right cheap.'

'Well let's face it, is it no' better that, than them coming tae the door tae complain about me growling, or biting them?'

He had a point, so I paused to think for a moment.

'I suppose, but just so long as you keep away from any more bitches about here that might be in heat. That couple looking after that big Afghan hound from Clarkston will never forgive you for running away with her!' I reminded him.

'Here! That's nothing, big man,' he said, before adding, 'Just wait till ye see the surprise they're about tae get in the next few weeks. Beautiful long-haired Afghans wi' wee short legs. I'd love to be a fly on the wall when they try to explain that to her owners!'

'Here, Harry, can ye put that on my Kennel Club CV? Wee Jockarusso the Yorkshire Terrier! Kennel Club registered. Pedigree name: "The Cock of the North"!'

Since this story has been written, Wee Jock has managed to secure an Equity acting / performers card.

As a result, he has been offered the lead in the remake of *Greyfriars Bobby*, but he has turned the offer down flatly, preferring to play the collar instead!

The Examination

. . .

A beautiful young policewoman made an appointment to see the chief medical officer.

She was only in the waiting room a few minutes when the medical officer called her in.

As she entered his room, he took one look at her gorgeous slim, model-like figure, coupled with her film-star beauty, and all his professionalism flew right out the window. He immediately instructed her to remove all her clothing.

Without the slightest hesitation, she disrobed, and he began to examine her, stroking her bare thighs. Whilst doing this he asked her, 'Do you know what I am checking for by doing this?'

'Yes,' she replied. 'You're checking me out for any abrasions or dermatological abnormalities on my legs.'

'That's exactly what I'm checking for!' said the medical officer, as he then changed position and began to caress and fondle her perfectly formed breasts.

'Do you know what I am doing now?' he asked her.

'Yes,' she said. 'I presume you are checking for any lumps which might indicate early signs of breast cancer.'

'You're perfectly correct in your presumption,' replied the amorous medical officer.

Finally, he got onto the couch beside her and within seconds he began to make passionate love to her.

'Do you have any idea what I might be doing now?' he asked her.

To which she replied, 'Yes! You're getting a right dose of the crabs, which is what I came to see you about in the first place.'

Public Complaints

· · ·

These are genuine clips from British council house tenants complaining to their local councils about problems with their houses.

1. My bush is really overgrown round the front and now my back passage has fungus growing out of it. I'm disgusted.

2. It's the dog's mess that I find the hardest part to swallow.

3. I want to complain about the farmer across the road. Every morning about 5 a.m. his cock wakens me up and it's now becoming too much for me to take.

4. I am a single woman living alone in a downstairs flat and I want you to please do something about the noise made by the young man who is on top of me every night banging away.

5. My neighbour's sixteen-year-old son is forever banging his balls against my fence. I'm becoming frustrated with it.

7. Please could you send a man round with the right tool to finish the job, and finally satisfy my wife once and for all.

8. My toilet seat is cracked, where do I stand?

9. I am writing this letter to you on behalf of my sink, which is coming away from the wall and leaking water.

10. Will you please send someone to mend the garden path? My wife tripped and fell on it yesterday and now she is pregnant with our first child.

11. I'm writing to you in order to have your permission to remove my drawers in the kitchen, because they are loose and falling down all the time.

Public Complaint
• • •
Fifty per cent of the walls in council houses are damp, fifty per cent have crumbling plaster and another fifty per cent are just plain filthy.

The Hoover Man

· · ·

Yesterday, my elderly mother opened her front door to a well-dressed young salesman holding onto a fancy-looking cylinder vacuum cleaner.

'Good morning, Mrs Morris,' said the young man. 'If I could take a couple of minutes of your time, I would just like to demonstrate to you the very latest, top-of-the range, high-powered vacuum cleaner.'

'No thanks, son!' she said. 'I've absolutely no money left. I'm totally skint!'

At that, she went to close the front door over.

Quick as a flash, the brash young salesman wedged his foot in her door and prevented it from closing.

'Don't be too hasty, Mrs Morris!' he said. 'Not until you have at least seen my miraculous demonstration.'

With that, he proceeded to empty a bucket of dog poo, cigarette butts and everyday crap all over her hallway carpet.

'Now, if this vacuum cleaner cannot remove all traces of this disgusting mess I have just deposited over your carpet, I will personally eat whatever is left over.'

At that, my mother stepped back and said, 'Well son, I've enjoyed your sales pitch, but I just hope you've got a bloody good appetite, because an engineer from Scottish Power disconnected my electricity this morning. As I explained to you earlier, I'm totally skint, so I couldn't pay my bill!

Now, would you like a glass of water with that?'

The Glesca Ned

...

The train about to leave Euston station for Glasgow Central was quite crowded, so the young Glesca ned walked the entire length of the coach looking for a seat. The only seat left was taken by a well-dressed middle-aged sophisticated woman's wee Yorkshire terrier dog, with a pink ribbon on its head.

The young Glesca ned had just completed a twelve-hour shift at a rave and was totally knackered, so he politely asked, 'Scuse me, doll face, but can I huv that seat yer wee dug's sittin' oan? I need tae rest ma pins, Ah'm knackered.'

The well-dressed woman ignored his plea, and turning her head, she said to no-one in particular, 'The young men of today are so scruffy and rude. My little Tina is occupying that seat.'

The young ned ignored her remark and defused the situation by walking the entire length of the train once again, but the only seat available was under Tina the Yorkie dog. So back he came.

'Please, missus, can Ah sit doon on that seat? Ah'm totally buggered, hen, and I'm wilting efter been oan a high wi' eckies.'

She snorted. 'Not only are you extremely rude, but you are also extremely arrogant!'

This time the young ned didn't say a word, he just bent down, picked up the little Yorkie dog, opened the window and tossed it off the train onto the platform, then sat down in the vacant seat.

The woman shriekcd, 'Aarrghh! Somebody do something about this! Put this young thug in his place!'

At that, an elderly English gentleman sitting nearby spoke up. 'Son, you young men from Scotland seem to have a penchant for doing the wrong thing. You don't speak the Queen's English very well, and you certainly don't seem to be very good at decision making. And as a result of the latter, son, you appear to have thrown the wrong bitch out of the train window!'

The Credit Crunch

• • •

The credit crunch continues to bite deeper and make noticeable holes in our savings and share issues. Everywhere you turn, it's doom and gloom, but it doesn't have to be and to prove it here are a few wee tips to hopefully cheer you up, or keep you from running to the bathroom for the razor blades.

This little scenario full of wisdom was sent to me by one of my good friends, and I think it was meant to cheer me up.

You see, according to him, if you had been adventurous with your investments and purchased £1000 of Northern Rock shares one year ago, it would now be worth a staggering £4.95.

With HBOS, earlier this year, your £1000 investment would have been worth an amazing £16.50, and the same £1000 invested in XL Airways would now be worth less than £5.

However . . .

If you had invested your money wisely and purchased £1,000 worth of Strongbow cider one year ago, and over a short period of time drank the lot, then taken the empty cans over to an aluminium recycling plant, you would be £214 better off.

So based on the above statistics, the best current investment advice available to us all is to drink heavily and then recycle the container that it came in.

He then offered me these words of advice: 'Remember, Harry, I used to be a teller in the UK's largest bank, so I know about stuff like this.'

Oh, and as an added incentive for drinking all this cider? He confirmed that the apples fermented to make Strongbow will count as one of your five-a-day fruits for a fit and healthy lifestyle.

'You know what? I'm feeling better already!'

Bath Night
...

A couple take in a young nineteen-year-old girl as a lodger.

The following day she asked if she could take a bath. The woman landlord informed her that they didn't have a bathroom, but if she liked she could use a tin bath in front of the fire.

'A Monday would be the best night, that's when my policeman husband goes out early on nightshift duty,' she said.

The girl agreed to have a bath on Monday.

A few days later, on the Monday, after the landlord's husband had gone out early on police duty, the woman filled the tin bath and watched with interest as the young girl got undressed.

She was surprised to see that she didn't have any pubic hair.

The following morning, the landlord couldn't wait to tell her husband, when he returned home from his night duty.

The husband didn't believe her, so she said, 'I'll tell you what then, next week, when she's having her bath, I'll leave a gap in the room curtains so that you can see for yourself.'

The following Monday, after the husband had gone out on duty, the young girl was getting undressed to have her bath.

The landlord asked her, 'Do you shave yourself downstairs?'

'No,' replied the girl. 'I've just never managed to grow any hairs down there. Why? Do you have hair down there?'

'I certainly do,' said the landlord and she lifted her skirt to show off her thicket of pubic hair.

The following morning, when her husband arrived home from duty, she asked, 'Well! Did you see it?'

'Of course I saw it,' he replied. 'But why the hell did you have to go and show her yours?'

'Why not?' she said. 'It's not as if you haven't seen it all before.'

'I know that,' he said, 'but all the boys on my bloody shift hadn't!'

The Fur Coat

· · ·

One night shift while on beat patrol, Alex was approached by a disgruntled male who wanted to make a complaint regarding the 'red-light district' girls.

He explained that he had met with a female wearing a fur coat, whom he alleged had approached him and offered, for an agreed fee, her sexual services in a nearby lane.

She was wearing a suspender belt under her coat and insisted on having anal sex only, using a condom and KY jelly.

If that didn't arouse his suspicion, I think he tells porkies!

However, he continued relating his story, where in the latter stages of heated passion he put his hands around her front, and to his total surprise (aye right) grabbed a big pair of hairy balls!

After the sex, he demanded his money back, claiming fraud.

He/She told him to 'Go forth and multiply!' (Polite version.)

As far as the police were concerned, it was a civil matter and as a verbal contract had been agreed, there could be no police action.

However, he insisted in pursuing his complaint of fraud, so Alex suggested that he notify his wife of his where-abouts and to come and uplift him at the police station, where his statement was being noted. This offer was immediately declined.

After some lengthy talks, where it was explained to him the can of worms he could be opening for himself unless he considered withdrawing his complaint, he agreed and left.

About an hour later, another patrol car saw a person fitting the description of him/her in a fur coat entering a city centre lane.

A police whistle was blown but he/she managed to make good his/her escape on bare feet, after removing his/her high heels.

Information and a description of him/her was passed to the Vice Squad, but he/she never returned to the red-light area again.

Well, let's just say they never received any other complaints!

Beam Me Up!

· · ·

Last week was my colleague's birthday and he wasn't feeling very well when he woke up that morning and went downstairs for breakfast, hoping his wife would be excited and welcome him with a big 'Happy Birthday' and surprise him with a present.

As it turned out, she paid him no attention whatsoever, let alone wish him a happy birthday.

He thought to himself, 'That's marriage for you, but at least the kids will remember and come rushing in with their presents.'

Unfortunately for him, his kids came down for breakfast and never uttered a word in his direction.

As a result, when he left that day to go on duty, he was feeling low and very despondent.

He parked his car and was walking across the car park to the rear of the police station, when Barbara, a detective constable on his shift said, 'Good morning, boss, and happy birthday!'

He felt good, knowing that someone had remembered.

He worked that day until two p.m. and then Barbara knocked on his office door and said, 'Excuse me, boss, I was wondering, as it's such a beautiful day outside and it's your birthday, can I take you out to lunch – just you and me?'

'Why thank you, Barbara,' he replied. 'That would be wonderful.' And grabbing his coat, he said, 'Let's go!'

Off they went to lunch, but they didn't go to one of the local restaurants, instead she took him to a discreet little diner with a private table and ordered up Martinis.

They drank them down and enjoyed the meal tremendously.

On the way back to the office, Barbara said, 'You know, it's such a beautiful day. Do we really have to go back to the office?'

He thought for a moment before replying, 'I suppose not, why, what do you have in mind?'

'Let's go to my apartment!' she suggested.

'Okay!' he responded.

When they arrived at her apartment, Barbara turned to him and said, 'Boss? If you don't mind, I'm going into the bedroom for a moment, but I'll be right back.'

'Yeah, no problem, Babs,' he replied nervously.

At that, Barbara disappeared into the bedroom, and after a few minutes, reappeared carrying a huge birthday cake lit up with candles, closely followed by his wife, his kids, his friends and several members of the CID officers from his shift, all singing 'Happy Birthday' to him.

He was totally stunned and shocked as he sat on the sofa, nervously focussing on everyone present in the room, while they looked on in surprise at him sitting there, totally naked!

Taxi Fare

...

My brother Hughie was driving his taxi one night when he picked up a hire going to Pollok.

'I've no' got any cash on me, mate, but if you stoap at a hole in the wa' bank on the way, I'll get some dosh out to pay ye!'

'Well it's twenty-five pounds for the fare,' said Hughie.

'Nae problem, mate, I'll just lift thirty quid to cover yer tip!'

Hughie duly pulled in at an automated cash machine on the way and his passenger got out and went over to it.

Moments later he got back in and said, 'That machine isnae working, mate. I'll show ye one nearer the hoose, it's handy.'

The passenger engaged in conversation with Hughie as he continued to convey him along the road to his destination.

Suddenly the passenger said, 'Stoap here at the next corner, big man, there's a bank hole just across the road there. I'll go tae that one and get yer dosh for ye!'

Hughie duly obliged and his passenger got out of the taxi, ran across the road to the cash machine and continued running, straight past it, around the corner out of sight and promptly disappeared from view, never to be seen again!

Missing, Presumed Pished!

• • •

Back in the City of Glasgow Police in the 1960s, alcohol was readily available to the police of all ranks by a more than generous Glesca public, and pub landlords.

As a result of this, a cop on each shift would be delegated the task of searching for any missing cops, during their tour of duty.

The cop detailed to perform this duty would report directly to a certain superintendent, who after submission of a report would ascertain whether it was classed as internal or, if any member of the public was involved, the incident would be referred to police headquarters.

One particular nightshift, Joseph Cassidy went missing whilst working the Glasgow Cross beat and an inquiry was set up to trace his whereabouts.

Several hours later, Joe was traced to the police stables in Bell Street, drunk as a lord, snuggled up, fast asleep, alongside Glenda the police horse, who he claimed was his best pal and fully understood him.

Unbeknown to Joe, while he was rolling about the hay with Glenda and presumed missing in action, his fellow colleagues on night shift had been retained on duty until his whereabouts were confirmed and he was found.

As it was, this was the last straw for Joe, with one disciplinary incident involving alcohol too many.

After some lengthy discussions with the superintendent, Joe was required to hop along and resign from the polis forthwith.

However, for the sake of all you animal lovers out there,

let me just say, no animals were injured during the actual events or the writing of this story, but Glenda was severely reprimanded and warned regarding her future conduct!

Now let me make you aware of another, more serious, incident involving Charlie!

It occurred on the late shift, when Charlie, a popular figure with the superintendent, went missing.

This coincided with an emergency call being received, regarding a police officer requiring urgent assistance at a tenement house address, near to Bridgeton Cross.

On arrival at the house, the attending officers found Charlie in the uncompromising position of being naked from the waist down, and wielding his police baton about wildly, striking a male suspect about the head and body.

During the formal investigations, the officers discovered that the suspect male was the innocent party here, and was actually the complainer, witness, reporter, victim and householder.

It further transpired that the complainer had unexpectedly returned home from his work place, to discover a half-naked Charlie in bed, engaged in sexual intercourse with his wife.

As a result, a disturbance ensued within the household.

However, due to Charlie's blatant refusal to put down his baton, coupled with his continual violent behaviour towards the husband and the officers in attendance, he was handcuffed and charged with breach of the peace, serious assault and police assault, before being conveyed to Tobago Street police station.

At this point, I should confirm that this was a pre-Viagra period, and that it *was* his police baton he was wielding about!

As for the husband, due to the injuries he sustained, he was conveyed to the Glasgow Royal Infirmary, where he was diagnosed with a fractured skull and two broken fingers.

Charlie was suspended from duty, to await his trial date.

However, Charlie did not have to wait long, because as luck would have it – and we're talking winning-the-Lottery type luck here – the court case against him was deserted by the Crown!

Charlie's luck didn't end there: several months after his return to full police duty, he was promoted sergeant! I must have missed that entire section in the police manual.

Anyways, you can only get away with it for so long, then your past catches up with you, and for Charlie, it didn't take long before he was at it again and required to resign this time.

Good Spirit

...

Two retired old cops, Sid and Bill, have been friends for most of their lives, having also worked together as police officers.

When it was discovered that Bill was dying, Sid made a house visit to him every day. During one of his visits, Sid said, 'Bill, we've both loved rugby all our lives, and we've played rugby together for the Glesca polis for many years.

'Please do me one favour, when you get to heaven, try and make contact with me and let me know if they play rugby up there.'

Bill looked up at Sid from his death bed and said, 'Sid, you've been my best friend for many years. If it's at all possible, I'll contact you somehow and let you know.'

A few days later, as expected, old Bill succumbed to his ill health and passed away in his sleep.

Several weeks later, while tucked up in his bed, Sid was awakened from a deep sleep by a blinding flash of white light and a familiar voice called out to him, 'Sid! Sid!'

'Who's that?' asked Sid, sitting up in bed. 'Who's there?'

The voice replied, 'Sid, it's me, it's Bill.'

'You're not Bill. Bill passed away a few weeks ago.'

'I'm telling you, it's me, Sid,' insisted the voice.

'Bill! Is it really you? Where are you?'

'I'm up in heaven,' replied Bill. 'I have some really good news for you, and a little bad news.'

'Well, tell me the good news first,' said Sid.

'Right!' replied Bill. 'The good news is there's rugby being played up here in heaven, and even better still, all of our old polis colleagues and team mates who've died before us are up here as well. But better than that, we're all younger guys again.

'And better still, it's always spring time up here and it never rains or snows. And the best thing of all is, we play rugby all day, every day, for as long as we want and we never get tired.'

'That's absolutely fantastic,' said Sid. 'It sounds better than I could ever have imagined. So tell me, what's the bad news?'

To which Bill replied, 'Your name's on the team sheet for Tuesday's game.'

The Original PC

· · ·

A friend of mine sent me some facts about the original PC, and when I say the original PC, we're not talking Robert Peel here. No, we are talking about the modern, everyday, much needed office and home accessory: the computer and some of the fancy new jargon that is associated with it. Let me furnish you with some examples:

Memory was something you lost the older you got.

Application was what you made to an employer, when asking for a job.

Programme was usually a family TV show such as *Sunday Night at the London Palladium*.

Cursor was someone who continually used bad language.

Keyboard was a piano or fancy organ.

Web was what a spider weaved.

Virus was usually a dose of the flu.

CD was a nickname for your bank account.

Hard drive was a long journey on the road.

Mouse pad was where a mouse lived.

And, last but not least, if you had a **3" Floppy**, that was usually the result of having just enjoyed a bloody good night!

Viagra!

• • •

Wee Carol made an appointment with her GP to ask his advice about reviving her husband Shuggie's libido.

'What about trying Viagra?' suggested her doctor.

'Viagra? No way!' she said. 'He won't even take an Aspirin.'

'Not a problem,' replied the doctor. 'Just give it to him when he isn't looking!'

'How do I do that?' asked Carol.

'Simple!' said the doctor. 'You slip it into his coffee. He won't even taste it. Give it a try and call in and see me in a week to let me know how things went.'

A week later, she called at the surgery to see the GP, who immediately enquired how it had gone.

Carol replied that it had been terrible!

'Terrible?' asked the doctor. 'Why? What happened?'

'Well, I did exactly what you suggested and slipped it into his coffee. The effect was almost immediate. Shuggie sprung up from his seat at the table, with a twinkle in his eyes and a bulge in his pants. With one swoop of his arm, he sent the cups and tablecloth flying from the table. He then grabbed hold of my blouse and skirt, ripping them off me, and took me there and then, holding me passionately down, we had a table-ender. It was a bloody nightmare, and I mean a nightmare!'

'Why was it such a nightmare?' the doctor asked. 'Are you saying the sex wasn't very good?'

'Are you off your head? It was the best spontaneous, raucous sex I've ever had with him in thirty years of married life! But as sure as I'm standing here, we'll never, ever be able to show our faces back in the Asda cafeteria ever again!'

Marriage

. . .

If you decide that your wife isn't treating you right, remain married anyway, because as sure as hell, there is no better way of punishing her.

Whisky Fruit Pies

. . .

HARRY'S RECIPE!
>One pint of filtered water.
>Two dessert spoons of sugar (or honey).
>Four nobs of butter (or one big lump).
>One big skoosh of lemon juice, hand squeezed.
>Six large free-range eggs (caged if you can't find them).
>One packet of cashew nuts.
>Two cups of dried fruit.
>Two bottles of Whyte & Mackay whisky (or more).

Sample the whisky in a large glass just to check the texture and the quality of the mature blend.

Take a large bowl, and before you do anything, just check the quality of the other bottle of whisky (a second opinion also helps to guarantee you have made the right choice, so try again).

Pour yourself a good measure and swallow it straight down.

Oh, lovely! What a good choice.

Right! Switch on the electric mixer (remember to plug it in).

Beat up eight ounces of butter in a large bowl.

Add one teaspoon of cake essence and set about it again.

At this point, it is advisable to check that the whisky is still okay, so pour yourself another good measure.

Turn off the mixer thingy and break two legs and add to the bow before chucking away the dried fruit.

Pick up some of the dried fruit off the floor and do what you want – you can eat it as part of your fifteen a day!

Mix the turner on, and if anything gets stuck in the beaters, use a drew scriver to pry them lose. Hic!

Oops, sorry about that. Hic! I think I've Hic! Got the Hic!

I better open the second bottle of whisky again to check its tonsisticity, hold your breath for thirty minutes, then sift two spoonfuls of salt . . . Salt? Where did the salt come from?

Actually, I think it means malt! Talking about malt, I better check the whisky again.

Shift the lemon juice and strain your nuts, then add a table!

Add a drop of sugar, or was it salt? Add to paste or whatever, I'm not very sure, but hey it's 'Christmas wine, thistletoe and slime'. Burrpp! Ooops, sorry! Wee bit o' windy pops there.

Make some toast. That's it, make a toast and pour yersel' another hauf. Cheers!

BUMP! Oh ya bugger, that was sore, but 'Pick yourself up, dust yourself off and start all over again.' Cheers!

Right! What have we not used yet?

Now, at this point, it's a good ikea to pour a wee whisky!

Oh, I remember now, you greash the oven and burn the cake tin to 360 degrees, trying not to fall over, 'cause it's very slippy in there and I've already got a big lump on my napper.

Crikey! There's rabbit shit all over the bloody floor!

False alarm! I've just tasted it. It's only raisins.

Whit noo? Oh aye, very impotent. Add a desperate spoon of whisky to the stuffy mix.

If you haven't got a spoon, just spit in about a mouthful, but not a full mouthful. Ye don't want to waste guid whiksy.

A bit of advice here. Don't eat any of the nuts before you do this, 'cause it's a waste of catch-ewes! And makes one a helluva mess. Looks like some pebble dash has been spilt all o'er it.

So, remember, it's a mouthful of whiksy and gargle it first.

Don't want tit to be too wet, so swallow it for good luck.

Now, for goodness' sake, don't forget to thingy, you know, 'cause every bugger I tell always forgets to do that. Even me!

Finally, pour the fish bowl through the window, finish off the reminder of the booze and make sure ye stuff the oven in the dishwasher before ye pass out on the floor.

Ye now what wormen are like if ye leaf a mess in their pre– pre– pre– How do ye spell precious? In their kitchen.

PS, I've newer massaged to cake a make vet, but it sounds lick somethink I'd really enploy!

CHERRY MISTMAS VERYDOBY! HIC!

And a Harry 'F' word to Goradon Rasmay. Ya big diddy!

It's How You Say It!
...

During a holiday break in Spain, the missus and I were in a busy pub restaurant that was serving up roast beef and Yorkshire pudding for lunch.

Due to this being on the menu, the pub was fairly busy with holiday punters.

The waitress's name was Syrita and she was very competent as she served all the tables inside as well as outside on the promenade, but it was most noticeable that each time she came inside to collect an order for outside, she was openly flirting with a shaven-headed Spanish male seated at the next table to us, and throwing lollipops at him, which he would readily catch.

In conversation, my missus asked if they were an item, but it appeared they weren't, and that he was just a local Spanish lad who had always drank there.

Although the female waitress had a broad Bradford accent, she was fluent in her Spanish, and could also have easily passed for a local, due to her sallow skin colour.

'How long have you lived here in Spain?' my missus asked.

'Five years!' she promptly replied.

'Five years?' my wife repeated. 'Is he your boyfriend?' she asked, referring to the shaven-headed Spaniard.

'No! I'm married to an Englishman. My hubby arrives back today from England. But Pepe here is a good friend – and hot, hot, hot! Mind you, I'd love to suck the face off of him!' she unashamedly announced.

My missus laughed at her actions, before asking her seriously, 'Is there any Spanish in you, Syrita?'

To which Syrita looked over at Pepe rather flirtatiously, threw him another lollipop and said, 'No! But I wouldn't mind some!'

Fly Guy!

...

Prior to retiring from the police, one of the last organised office parties I attended with my shift was a real special occasion. Not only was it an excellent three-course meal, but also included on the night was some first-class live entertainment, provided by a superb female impersonator/singer.

After our meal, due to a well-funded kitty, the drinks were arriving thick and fast at our table and were being consumed as rapidly as they were being poured.

Eventually, due to the amount of liquid being drunk, along with a few colleagues, I required to make a visit to the toilet. On our return, the female entertainer was singing a lively Tamla Motown number and the rhythm, coupled with the alcohol we'd consumed, got us moving to the beat and attempting to dance with her.

The female singer seemed to approve of our intervention and our attempt to join in and get involved with her music, and began to interact with us all, dancing along with us.

Then after a few moments, she sidled up towards me, moving wonderfully to the beat, and singled me out to dance with her as, one by one, the other guys dejectedly sat back down at the table to watch how it was done.

I felt like someone special to be picked out by her, and was even beginning to believe that somehow, overnight, having only watched a few episodes of *Strictly Come Dancing*, I had gone from being shite to champagne, as far as my dancing skills were concerned.

As she moved effortlessly to the beat, whilst still singing and dancing, she leaned forward, put her hand behind my head, pulled me towards her, and whispered into my ear, 'You seem like a very nice man, so when you get a minute . . . pull up your zip, love!'

On my return to the table, all the guys were desperate to know what the singer had whispered in my ear.

However, I decided it was better to keep schtum and let their inebriated imaginations run wild. After all, their individual versions sounded much better than the real truth!

Pick 'N' Mix Affairs

• • •

When America's queen of pop, Madonna, first moved to the UK, she immediately informed everyone in the media that more than anything, she wanted to meet the perfect Guy, 'Fit right in with the locals, and feel more like the everyday English housewife!'

Well after only seven years, she is now an unmarried single mother with three children, from three different fathers . . . .

And what about the Swedish beauty Ulrika Jonsson, a former weather presenter and TV host, who arrived on these shores several years earlier with the same dream of being an everyday housewife, who would fit right in and be readily accepted.

She's gone one better and has four children to one, two, three different fathers, as well as being renowned for being a mad shagger and having a few high-profile celebrity affairs.

Congratulations, girls, for having achieved your aim. Sounds like a job well done to me and I don't think it will be long before some bampots in our society nominate you to the Queen for some type of award!

Well why not? Frankie Dettori got one for having seven different mounts on the trot!

Dead Funny. Not!

• • •

Every Monday morning at 0800 hours in 'A' Division, Glasgow, it was the duty of the early shift inspector, armed with his clip board, to detail certain police officers, whom he issued with pro-forma 'sudden death' reports, to attend the homeless hostel at Holm Street and the Great Eastern Hotel in Duke Street, and note the identities and details of those who had unfortunately passed away over the weekend.

Craig was 'puppy' walking a brand-new young probationer called Campbell Baxter.

With a name like Campbell Baxter, it was little wonder that the shift automatically nicknamed him 'Two Soups'!

Two Soups was a big teuchter from South Uist, and had never seen a dead sheep, never mind a dead body, in his albeit short lifetime.

They were summoned to attend Holm Street, regarding the sudden death of one of its regular 'down and out' resident dossers.

On their arrival, Craig spoke with the reporter alone, who told him that the deceased had been found dead in the early hours of the morning, after which Craig rejoined his young colleague and began to instruct Two Soups on the police procedure and information he would require for his police report.

Like the full identity details of the victim.

Check for any sign of life.

Was the body still warm?

Was there any sign of physical abuse?

Note a description and take possession of all the deceased property and clothing.

After which, a request would be made for the attendance of the police casualty surgeon.

Two Soups looked at the dead body lying there and, immediately, the colour began to visibly drain from his face, to such an extent that the deceased looked healthier than him!

He took one step back, waved his hands away and point blank refused to look any more, let alone touch the deceased body.

Craig attempted to guide him and coerced him into putting his hand onto the neck of the deceased, claiming that he was positive that he detected a pulse.

After much persuasion and coaxing by Craig, he eventually convinced Two Soups to reach out with his hand and check for himself, which he did, rather half-heartedly.

'See. I told you. Quick!' announced Craig ecstatically. 'He's still alive. We'll need to resuscitate him. You apply mouth to mouth to him, while I massage his heart!'

These were the last words that Two Soups needed to hear while suffering from severe nausea, but Craig's enthusiasm to try to resuscitate the deceased male appeared to be genuine, and so the effort to do so had to be made.

Having recently taken a first-aid course at the police college, and fully aware of what action to take, Two Soups reluctantly locked lips with the foul mouth of the deceased.

Whilst seriously engaged in what he considered a real life-saving act and fully committed to the task, Craig immediately handcuffed him by the wrist, before attaching him to the arm of the deceased.

'You two look like you're getting on well, so I'll leave you to get better acquainted!' he smugly remarked as he left, locking the cubicle door, leaving a stunned and totally shocked Two Soups inside, joined at the wrist to the deceased with a pair of police handcuffs.

Poor Two Soups could be heard making noises like a new puppy left in the dark for the first time as he whimpered uncontrollably, while awaiting the arrival of the police casualty surgeon to pronounce life extinct.

However, moments prior to his arrival, Two Soups was released from his nightmare, ashen faced and uttering obscenities in his Gaelic tongue as he fled like an Olympic sprinter from the hostel, visibly upset at the actions of his wicked senior colleague.

Suffice to say, when Craig eventually caught up with him, hiding in the toilets of the police station, what had just occurred was not on the agenda for discussion – ever again!

Two Soups has now been retired for several years, but it is safe to say he will not have forgotten the day he was cruelly persuaded into performing mouth to mouth resuscitation to a dead body, and he certainly will never forgive his partner Craig for his actions on that day.

As it was, it didn't take long for him to be given a second nickname: 'Bondage Boy'.

This came about whenever he was asked at anytime

during the rest of his entire career to attend a report of a sudden death, when he would immediately respond with the reply, 'I'm sorry but I can't. I'm tied up at the moment!'

As for Craig and the rest of the shift, they all found the incident 'dead funny' and the more police service that Two Soups accumulated, the more exaggerated the story became so that his up-and-coming younger colleagues would often refer to him as 'Hot Lips', having heard the latest version of how he sooked the face off a deceased dosser in a hostel!

Which reminds me of the time I was walking the beat with Donnie Henderson and he suddenly started coughing, during which he uttered the words, 'Harry, I think I've got something stuck in my throat! I can't breathe properly.'

'Are you choking?' I asked him.

To which Donnie replied, 'Naw, I'm frigging serious!'

Advent Calendars
• • •

Leading up to Christmas this year, I purchased an advent calendar from a Jehovah's Witness.

The first door I opened, there were two of them behind it!

We Know What He Meant

· · ·

One of the best-known officials who served on the bench in Scotland was Sheriff J. Irvine Smith, the man with a thousand witty responses and hilarious throwaway lines.

On one occasion he was within the court restaurant along with his court assistant, and looked across at two young girls, wearing very skimpy miniskirts on a cold, wet winter's day and allegedly remarked, 'If those two young girls don't cover up, they'll end up with chaps between their thighs!'

Quick Wit!

· · ·

A young blonde girl came running into a shop and said to her boyfriend, 'Jimmy! Somebody has just stolen your Range Rover from the car park!'

'Did you see who it was?' he asked her.

'No, he was wearing a ski mask, but I wrote down the registration number!'

Gerry, the police club manager, received an invoice that he couldn't quite work out, so he decided to obtain the assistance of Brenda, the new barmaid.

'Here, Brenda! You've done your Highers. If I was to give you £400 minus fifteen per cent, how much would you take off?'

Brenda thought for a moment before replying,

'Everything but my earrings!'
Traffic cops stopped a lorry driver in Govan, walked up to the driver's window and said, 'You got any ID?'

The driver replied, 'About what?'

Traffic cops see a driver dumping rubbish at the side of the road in a designated parking place and stop to speak with him.

'Why are you dumping rubbish in the parking place? Can't you read the notice?' they asked.

'Yes I can read,' he replied. 'That's why I'm dumping it here, because it specifically says "FINE FOR DUMPING RUBBISH"!'

A retired cop was overheard saying, 'When the world officially comes to an end, I want to be in Lesmahagow, Scotland!'

'Why?' asked his pal.

'Because everything in Lesmahagow happens ten years after the rest of the country!'

Horse Talk

• • •

Sandy was on early shift, covering four beats in the Calton area, when at about 0930 hours he received a radio call to attend at Turnbull Street, near the Central police station, regarding the report of a saddled horse wandering about outside Ben Parsonage house in the Glasgow Green.

The horse was found and led by a member of the public to the Central police office and was in the care of the civilian car washer in the back yard.

It was immediately identified as a police horse minus its police rider.

Knowing the beat well, Sandy made his way along to the Saltmarket and visited a popular local public house, where lo and behold, he came across another police horse minus its rider, which was loosely tied up to a fence at the rear, with its head hanging over an iron gate, looking slightly lost.

However, after some initial police enquiries, it was revealed that by pure coincidence, both police riders required to use the toilet at the same time and thereby tethered their horses out of the view of the public.

Subsequently, once inside, they were offered some free hospitality and settled down for a light refreshment, unbeknown to them that one of their horses had broken loose while awaiting their return and decided to wander off all by itself.

Their feeble excuse was accepted, as both police riders were reunited with their stray horses and no report was ever submitted. Not even a 'Visit to Licence Premises' form.

By the way, I'm guaranteed they were definitely not drinking 'White Horse' whisky.

Aye right!

Next you'll be telling me they were in there to use the toilet?

What's in a Name?

• • •

In these modern days where we are more and more governed by the intervention of political correctness, you cannot be too careful, but you can be perceived as being over sensitive.

An armed robbery took place at a street corner shop in Govan, owned by an Asian family.

After the initial response and noting of the incident by the attending officers who were first on the scene, a civilian member of the Scenes of Crime department was requested to attend.

A crime scene officer attended and reported that he had dealt with the incident at the 'Guptas' corner shop.

On seeing the message on his desk, the SOC inspector drafted a letter to the crime officer, commenting that he had just read over his report and was of the opinion that his derogatory description of the shop owner was uncalled for and not one bit funny, and furthermore, he wanted an explanation regarding same.

The crime officer was confused and reported back that he had described the corner shop as the 'Guptas' because the family name was Gupta!

The SOC inspector was unaware of this and on seeing the report citing the word 'Guptas', he had assumed it to be a slighting reference to the Asian family who owned the shop.

To make matters worse, the SOC inspector conveyed his apologies to the civilian crime officer, Mister Blackhead!

Wrong again, Inspector, his name was Whitehead, and he was not amused at the name change!

Mind you, makes you wonder what the inspector was thinking about when he wrote his apology?

American Dragnet Stories

• • •

Police officers in California, USA, spent two hours attempting to subdue an armed gunman who had barricaded himself inside his house.

After firing ten tear gas canisters through the windows and getting no response from the gunman, the officers discovered that the man was standing beside them in the police line, shouting, 'Come outside and give yourself up!'

A man pretending to be armed with a gun kidnapped a motorist and forced him to drive to two different automated teller machines, whereby the kidnapper proceeded to withdraw money from his own account.

Police in Los Angeles had good luck with a robbery suspect who just couldn't control himself during a police line-up. When detectives asked each man in the line-up to repeat the words 'Give me all your money or I'll shoot', the suspect male stepped forward, rather irate, and said, 'That's not what I shouted!'

A man walked into an Eight Till Late store and ordered the assistant to hand over all the money in the cash drawer.

However, the cash amount was so small that he tied up the assistant and proceeded to serve at the counter himself for three hours until he had earned enough to rob it.

Steven Richard King was arrested by the police when he tried to hold up a Bank of America branch, without a weapon.

Apparently King, with his hand concealed inside his coat pocket, used his thumb and forefinger to simulate a gun.

Unfortunately for him, he was overcome by staff, who realised he was unarmed when he failed to keep his hand in his pocket and started waving it about.

Gaetano

• • •

On my first trip to Italy it was my misfortune to meet the one and only gigolo / con-man of San Giovanni Rotundo.

There I was trying to look totally inconspicuous, mingling among the locals like a native of the area.

I was further convinced that I appeared nothing like your average everyday tourist, even with my Nikon 35mm camera dangling from my yellow luminous neck strap, my TK Maxx sunglasses, with label still attached, just in case I didn't suit them and required to take them back, along with my Scotland baseball cap with matching Saltire tee-shirt.

The exact opposite of what I had told the missus to wear, in order to fit right in and not to be noticed.

Suddenly, he appeared in front of me, dressed in a smart beige double-breasted suit (Italian, no doubt) with a neat collar and tie, a cashmere coat, neatly folded over his left arm, and last but not least, his Emporio Armani sunglasses, propped up on top of his balding head.

'*Scusilo per favore voi,*' he said, then made a sign with his hand to his mouth, signifying an eating motion.

I nodded my head and said, 'Yesso, we looking.'

'*Prego voi vengono!*' he said, beckoning us to follow him.

So, like two wee obedient Scottie dogs, desperate to please their master, we followed after him.

We followed him up a steep hill, along a narrow cobbled street, through another narrower street, by which point my police experience took over and I said to my missus, if he turns into one more narrow, dead-end street, I'm going to give him one almighty kick in the balls, so get ready to run!'

'Naw, don't, Harry, he looks like something out the Mafia!'

Now let me explain something right away. When abroad, I'm always suspicious of everyone, and at this particular moment in time, I think he's leading the 'stupid tourist' up the garden path to relieve them of their camera, mobile phones, wallet, watch and any other items of value, such as jewellery and, oh yes, their holiday Euros! (Not worth a lot these days.)

However, here we were being sucked up like a new carpet under attack from the latest James Dyson vacuum cleaner, all of which was being expertly carried out by a complete and total stranger in a foreign land.

I'm not sure if he heard my previous statement to my missus about kicking him in the balls, or just decided we had walked several kilometres and that enough was enough.

Suddenly, he came to an abrupt halt directly outside what appeared to be the front entrance door to a small house.

'*Qui! Qui!*' he announced, nodding his head at the same time, as if to signal our arrival at the restaurant.

With that, he grabbed a handful and pulled aside the long beaded drapes allowing us our first view of the inside.

'Oh this looks lovely, Harry, and there's even other people inside, and what do you know, there's Vito Corleone and his family sitting round a table eating.'

Then she added sarcastically, 'Crikey, I'm positive that's Al Pacino in the corner, sitting beside Robert De Niro! Quick, follow me and Gaetano.'

With our new guide Gaetano leading the way, we entered.

Once inside, Gaetano quickly selected a table for us all to sit at and pointed it out to the waitress.

'I hope he doesn't think I'm buying him a drink!' I said. 'Because, for a moment there, I thought he was leading us up the proverbial cobbled path to be mugged!'

'Oh, buy him a drink to say thank you, for goodness' sake. He's been really nice, and brought us to a lovely wee restaurant.' She then put her head to the side in a sympathetic way, making a statement, like only a woman can.

'Awright! Awright! I'll buy him a drink,' I said begrudgingly. 'But only the one!'

Mind you, before I had finished my reply, Gaetano had taken that option away from me, by taking it upon himself to order up a large carafe of the best house wine for our table.

Like the host for the night, he filled our glasses with the house vino, and we all toasted in unison, '*Ai nuovi amici* – To new friends!'

'Don't think so!' I murmured under my breath.

Then before I could utter the immortal words of Dame Vera Lynn ('We'll meet again . . . Not!'), Gaetano made his intentions clear by picking up the restaurant menu and thumbing his way through it.

'What the hell does think he's doing now?' I remarked.

'Oh stop picking faults in him, he's only looking

through it. He's probably going to order something nice that we'll like. I think he's trying to impress us 'cause we're tourists.' explained the missus.

'I'm all for him trying to impress us, but I'd prefer he used his own money! In fact, if you ask me, I'm more inclined to believe the word is "fleece" us,' I said, looking totally unconvinced by her explanation.

'Och, buy him his dinner, it'll not be that much, and he's a lovely guy, going out of his way to bring us all the way up here, when he was probably on his way home for his own lunch!'

I looked at her disbelievingly, before replying to her rant.

'You said buy him a drink! I bought him a drink. Now it's a case of let's buy him his dinner. Let's get him to fuck off!'

'Oh behave yourself, Harry Morris. After all, we're on our holidays!'

'Exactly, hen! We are. But he's not!' I replied.

Then the missus gave me another one of those looks. You know, the other look this time that says, 'Do what you're told. Or you'll be sleeping by yourself, in the bath, for the duration of the entire holiday!'

Having expertly read her facial expression, I responded with the words, 'Okay, babes!' I didn't want to spend any more time in the hotel bog, having already occupied it for several hours since arriving, due to the hotel's 'special meatball pasta dish' presently operating on my bowel system like a fast-acting laxative.

In the meantime, our Latin gigolo Gaetano had whipped out his mobile phone with adaptor attached, and plugged it into a socket within the restaurant, in order to charge it up.

One did not need to be a detective to work out why he was charging up his mobile phone in there.

However, before I could comment about it, up comes the first course, antipasti.

'Eat, eat!' He motioned invitingly, putting his hand to his mouth before adding, '*Prego, prego!*'

It's a massive dish for three to eat, and this is only a starter that he's ordered for us. Then he waves his hands, signaling he doesn't want any of it, while screwing up his face.

'This lot must be crap if he doesn't want to eat it!' I said.

'Oh, don't be ridiculous, Harry, he's obviously watching his figure and saving himself for the main course.'

Gaetano then summoned the waitress and said, '*Le bistecca e l'insalata verde!*' He pointed to himself.

All the time I'm thinking to myself, 'What's he ordering now? Are we sharing with another table, or what?'

It didn't take long to find out, as the missus and I ploughed our way through courgettes soaked in oil, spicy peppers in oil, wafer thin aubergines in virgin olive oil and cold cubed potatoes, soaked in extra virgin oil. There was also a basket of crusty bread to soak up any other oily slick substance we might have left on the plate, or spilled down the front of my shirt.

With that one starter, I reckon I had now consumed more oil than the average family car engine!

I found myself sliding off the seat and it was nothing to do with consuming too much vino!

Meantime, over came the waitress to present Gaetano with a beautifully cooked entrecote beef steak, accompanied by a separate bowl of fresh green salad – minus any oil, of course!

Speechless, I looked on at his choice of food with envy, when my silence was interrupted by the missus, who remarked, 'Look at him. He's such a lovely eater, isn't he?'

I looked her straight in the eyes and replied, 'And so am I when I'm getting fed for nothing!'

At that, Gaetano looked up at me and said, *'Bella, bella!'*

'Ah think he might have understood what you said there Harry, quick, tell him a joke.'

'Well I'm not surprised if he did understand me, he's been in our company long enough to learn our entire language!' I replied sarcastically.

'Just in case he did, we better talk eggy language,' she said.

'Eggy language? What eggy language?'

'Eggy language? You know, whegger egger yeggou gegging?'

'Egger deggon't theggink seggo deggarlegging!' I replied. 'He's a "Tally", and the speed at which we talk at, he probably thinks we're Romanian or Polish!'

'Look up. Here comes our dinner!' the missus announced.

As the waitress put it down in front of us, I focused on what was a large plate of white pasta and green leafy stuff – at a quick glance, totally bowfing!

I thought twice about interrupting Gaetano, as he was

totally engrossed, daintily munching away on his fine steak and sipping regularly from his filled glass of house wine, but my frustration got the better of me.

'Ho, Gaetano! What is this?'

'*Magnifico!*' he said, kissing his fingers. '*Bella, bella!*'

'Bella! Fucking bella! I don't think so. No likey. It looko very mucho like el crappo, so takey it awayo and binno.'

I amazed the missus, as I appeared to be picking up the lingo very quicko, and with a certain degree of fluency I might add!

Then she leaned over the table to Gaetano and said, 'Quick, Harry, get your camera out and take a picture of me and Gaetano.'

Take a picture? Aye right!

However, I reluctantly took the picture of a smiling Gaetano sitting alongside the missus, thinking that Interpol might be interested in a copy of his mugshot.

Minutes later, another two dishes arrived at our table, to be placed in front of us at the bequest of our Italian gigolo.

Now this course was edible, but dare I say it, nothing great, so I managed to eat about half of it before I became sickened of the taste, so I politely offered our guest a taste, but he wasn't interested, and resoundingly refused it with the shake of his hand, uttering something in Italian at the same time.

I'm sure it sounded like, 'No way, gringo, we Italians don't eat that shit!'

The plates were cleared away and we sat back in our seats to relax and allow our latest course to settle down.

Gaetano got up, walked over to a table with dishes on it and proceeded to help himself to what appeared to be large scoops of Haagen Dazs vanilla ice cream.

'Oh, check him out. He's got to be taking the piss; he's helping himself to ice cream now!' I said. 'He's getting really gallus now and thinks he doesn't even need to ask me.'

'That's not ice cream, Harry, it's mozzarella cheese!'

'Who cares? Mister Whippy or mozzarella, it's immaterial to him 'cause he's not paying for it!' I replied.

He had only just sat back down with his cheese, when lo and behold, the waitress appeared with two more dishes for us. This time it was langoustines, large shrimps and some other molluscs still in their shell looking up at me with one eye.

'No! No! No!' I said assertively.

'*Voi! Voi! Voi!*' responded Gaetano, adding, '*Bella! Bella!*'

The waitress placed them ever so invitingly on the table in front of us.

I must say they were really fresh, as the biggest of the three langoustines appeared to be fighting with the other two!'

'I'm going to burst!' exclaimed the missus.

'Aye, and I'm going to burst him, if one more dish appears on this table!' I reacted, showing my disapproval.

Then I turned my attention and addressed him. 'Ho, Gaetano! Notto moreo,' I said, drawing my hand across my throat in a cutting fashion, in order to get my point across.

He drew his lips upward and nodded his head as we crunched our way through the unwanted shellfish, killing off any thoughts they had of escaping.

We finished off and sat back in our chairs once again, only this time we were totally exhausted.

Then I heard Gaetano say to the waitress, '*Grappa, grazie!*'

Before I could respond, a bottle was placed on the table with three glasses. Gaetano immediately took hold of the bottle like the host and filled them to the top.

He then held his glass up for a toast and uttered something, while I did likewise and uttered the immortal words, 'Enough-enough-O!'

Then he called to the waitress, '*La fatura, prego!*'

The waitress came over and promptly produced the bill for the table, Gaetano made a feeble attempt to take out his wallet, but before he could open it, the missus interrupted. 'Not at all Gaetano. You put your money away, you're our guest. Harry will pay for it!'

There's a moment in life when you would like the ground to open up and swallow . . . your missus! This was that moment.

However, there was a surprise in store for us when we got outside the restaurant, as Gaetano invited us to follow him for a coffee.

He then proceeded to lead us all the way back down through the narrow cobbled streets, where we eventually arrived at an ice cream parlour.

As we entered, he motioned for us to take a seat, while he approached the glass display counter to order up three large cream-filled, booze-soaked rum babas, pointing to the exact ones he wanted, which also coincided with being the biggest.

Now, neither myself or the missus are 'sweet' people, but stuff that, as Gaetano was paying for it, I decided to make an exception and force myself.

Surprisingly, we both thoroughly enjoyed them and it appeared Gaetano enjoyed it also, because he went straight back up and ordered a selection of three other cream-filled, liquor-soaked desserts.

Like the previous treats, we forced ourselves to 'gub' them.

When Gaetano finished and arose from his seat, he looked over to the counter assistant, said '*Ciao*' and signaled for us to follow him out the parlour.

As we made to leave with Gaetano, without any money changing hands for the sweets, the assistant shouted out at him.

Gaetano stopped in his tracks, turned to face him and a heated exchange of words took place between them.

That was the cue for the missus and I to leave them to it and step outside into the street, while we awaited the outcome.

Suddenly, Gaetano appeared at the door, held up his hand to us, before walking over and entering a nearby auto-bank cubicle.

Minutes later, would you believe it, he reappeared waving his bank card . . . but minus any money.

He uttered something that resembled a 'hard luck' story, which we quickly interpreted as being, 'I'm totally skint!'

'Go in and pay it for him, Harry!' suggested the missus.

'Are you off your bloody head? I've just bought this guy his dinner, and paid for several extra dishes that he ordered that weren't even edible.' Then I added, 'So much for the gesture of him pulling out his wallet in the restaurant and making out as if he was going to pay. He read us like a book and I bet he's played that old con trick a few times.'

'Well maybe so, but go in and pay it anyway. He's all embarrassed. . . . .'

'And totally skint!' I reminded her.

Anyways, as it was, I went in, walked up to the front counter and handed over ten Euros to the assistant, who promptly nodded his head, said 'Di piu!' He held out his hand for more. So I hesitantly handed him another ten Euros. Again, he nodded his head and said, 'Di piu!' He wanted more of my money. After I was forced reluctantly to part with a third ten-Euro note, he nodded his head the opposite way and handed me two Euros change.

When I walked back outside, the wife asked me immediately, 'Did you pay it?'

'Pay it? Aye, I paid it – and the rest that he must have owed. Our new best pal, Marlon Brando here just cost me another twenty-eight Euros. Bloody dear rum babas! Are you sure there wasn't a pearl inside them?'

'Well cheer up, you can get your own back. He wants us to follow him to his house for a drink,' she said, trying to soften the blow, but at this point, a night out with Sophie Loren wouldn't have done that.

'Oh come on, he's offering you his hospitality and a drink!' she repeated.

I paused for a moment, playing hard to please, before saying, 'Well in that case, I'm about to change from pasta, to pastor, and as such I'm going to exorcise his house, making sure I empty it of all spirits inside his drinks cabinet – and don't you dare tell me I've had enough! Just let him tell me when there's nothing left!'

We then followed Gaetano once again as he led us down the winding, narrow streets to his house.

After a short walk, we finally arrived at his apartment block and he pressed a buzzer. Moments later, a dour-faced female looked over from a balcony. Gaetano shouted, '*Aperto, aperto,*' at her, while gesturing with his key. She then disappeared.

However her disappearance coincided with a buzzer sounding and Gaetano pushed on the entrance door to open it.

We followed him up the stairs to the top, where he then produced a key from his pocket and opened the front door to an apartment.

Once inside, I must admit, the house was very small but immaculate. He even opened his wardrobes to show off the inside. My missus was overly impressed with his uniformed rows of neatly ironed shirts, ties, trousers, jackets, and even his bloody socks.

'See! Would you look at that, Harry Morris, he uses proper hangers to hang his clothes up, not like you. You hang all your clothes on the bedroom floor!'

My immediate thought was, 'Guys like this let our sex down and make it unbearable for the rest of us.'

After the tour, Gaetano led us into his kitchen and proceeded to filter some fresh coffee.

'Ho, Marlon! Where's the boozeo? I don't want your coffee and my missus doesn't drinko it either. We're looking for a few bottles of your Vino Collapso, comprendi?'

Next thing, he produced three bottles of beer – that was the entire stock of booze in his household!

'Aaarrgghhh!'

While I was opening *my* three bottles of beer, Gaetano had taken the missus outside onto his roof garden, with a patio swing seat, which she immediately had to sit on.

'This is lovely, Gaetano, all that's missing is some nice music. Have you any nice musica?'

Gaetano pointed to the electric light, then drew his hand across his throat. '*Nessun potere di elettricita*,' he said, following that up with his two fingers imitating a pair of scissors. 'Notta powder!'

'No eccentric powder?' I said mockingly, shaking my head.

'*Voi, voi*,' he replied. 'Notta powder!'

'No power? So you can't play any musica?' she asked.

'Naw, hen! He doesn't have any eccentric powder at all! Hence the reason he was charging his mobile phone in the restaurant!' I responded. 'And why doesn't he have any electricity in the house? Because, surprise, surprise, he doesn't have any money!'

I had just finished speaking when Gaetano appeared

with a very small transistor radio and switched it on, but it didn't play – the reason being, it needed batteries, and batteries cost money!

Then the missus stupidly pointed to a makeshift BBQ he had over in the corner of his roof garden, which Gaetano immediately interpreted as a sign for us to eat again.

He disappeared inside, reappearing moments later with his jacket on and his camel coat neatly folded over his arm. He then signalled me to come with him to '*Il macellaio*'.

'Where? Who?' I asked.

'Butcher!' he said very clearly in English.

I put my hand up and said, '*Una momento!*' And turning to my missus I said, 'Get up out that seat, because Elvis is about to leave the building!'

Unaware of what Gaetano was now suggesting, in order to relieve us of 'mucho moreo Euros', the missus asked, 'Why are we leaving, darling, are you not having fun?'

'Fun! I'm having the time of my frigging life, however, of all the rich, affluent, well off, loaded Italians living in Italy, we had the misfortune to hook up with a guy who has no money, no electricity, no food, no drink, and, I would hazard a guess, no job!

'As a result of all these noticeable attributes that Gaetano holds in abundance, I suspect he is about to ask me to drop my holiday shorts to my ankles, in order for him to park his bike between the cheeks of my arse!

'Therefore, my love, using my twenty-nine years of police experience, and as a result of my subsequent findings, I'm not prepared to continue subsidising our Italian Mafia buddy any longer, so let's GTF, ASAP.'

As we walked out of the apartment block, Gaetano made to follow us, but I waved my hand at him and uttered the two most internationally understood words of all time to put someone off . . .

No! Not those two.

I actually said in my best Italian accent, '*Arrivederci!*' And waved to him goodbye.

At that, we made our own way back to our hotel, unaccompanied.

The following day, we had to make our way to the town centre, to check on the bus timetable.

Whilst standing there studying the bus chart, we heard a loud commotion coming from behind us and turned around to see our former Italian guide, Gaetano, fully animated and loudly arguing with the same counter assistant from the ice cream parlour that we had visited.

The argument became more heated with typical Italian-like gestures being made by both men.

There was a young guy standing at the bus stop nearby, so the missus approached and asked him, 'Excuse me, do you speak English?'

'A little bit,' he replied.

'The men behind us, can you hear what they are arguing about?' she asked.

The young guy listened for a moment and said, 'They are arguing because the smaller man is saying the man in the suit owes him money.'

With that, we said Grazie to the young guy and buggered off sharpish before Gaetano saw us!

The experience I gained meeting Gaetano during my trip to his country will stay with me forever.

Now, every time I look through a travel brochure and see the beautiful Italian city of Rome, I immediately equate it with the words Rip Off My Euros!

Hasta la Pasta baby!

You Can Be A Polis . . .

. . .

IF you have the bladder capacity to hold a minimum 15 pints.

IF you have restrained someone and it wasn't during a sexual experience.

IF you believe that 75% of people are a waste of space.

IF your idea of a good time is an armed robbery at a shift change over.

IF you find humour in other people's stupidity.

IF you call up for a warrant check on anyone who is remotely friendly toward you.

IF you believe that unspeakable evils will befall you if anyone says, 'God it's quiet today!'

IF whenever you phone someone, you ask them, 'Are you free to speak?'

IF you're the only sober person in the kebab shop.

IF you believe that drinking alcohol at seven o'clock in the morning seems perfectly normal.

IF when you mention vegetables, you're not referring to a food group.

IF your prisoner states, 'I have no idea how I got here' and neither have you!

IF you answer your phone with the words, 'Stand by unless urgent!' And end a conversation with 'Roger' and 'Over!'

IF you walk down the street looking at people as potential criminal intelligence submissions.

IF your partner tells you off for walking with your hands held together behind your back.

IF you are the only person you know who ever uses the word 'liaise' when you talk with your wife.

IF you regularly say, 'With all due respect, sir,' but mean nothing of the sort.

IF you have a nose that is finely tuned to the smells of cannabis, decomposition and stale body odour.

IF at least once every working day, you use the phrase, 'The job's fucked!'

Then there's a career for you in the police!

Harry Says, 'Share With Me!'

• • •

Former police officer Harry Morris and now the author of the popular 'Harry the Polis' series of books is planning to publish book number eight in the series of funny short polis stories.

Harry the Polis, 'There's Been a Murder'!

He would like to extend an invitation to all serving and retired polis, along with all F.S.O. staff, to contribute a story to future publications and allow the popular series to continue.

Stories must be of a humorous nature and can even be a short scenario of an incident that you would like the author to expand upon. (All characters' names will be changed.)

We are all very much aware of the seriousness and important side of the job, when serving the public, that's why the humour we enjoyed in our everyday police duties was a very important feature of our work.

So why not share it with your colleagues and the public by giving everyone a laugh, as opposed to reading about horrific day-to-day crimes that feature daily in the press and are forced upon us in the news. Everybody likes a right good laugh.

Just send stories, poems, anecdotes, jokes or tales to: harry@harrythepolis.com
Website: www.harrythepolis.com

The author will be sure to credit you with your submission. However, if you wish to remain anonymous, this will also be respected by the author. The main objective is not to make fun of the police, but to write about the humour we all enjoyed.

So why not start writing and let me hear from you? We all have a funny story we've been involved in, so why not share it?

All attempts are made to identify the author of any material submitted and used.

NEXT PUBLICATION IN THE SERIES: VOLUME 8

HARRY THE POLIS, 'THERE'S BEEN A MURDER!'

Thank You

• • •

I hope you enjoyed perusing this book of short stories in my latest 'Harry the Polis' series as much as I have enjoyed writing, editing and compiling.

To all my former colleagues, and those young and not so young, who will sign on for a career as future police officers, I would offer you this valuable advice: at all times, use common sense when dealing with a situation and never be afraid to show compassion and, most of all, use your discretion.

Lastly, if you can't laugh at yourselves, then you should leave the job to others – like me and my readers, of course!

Acknowledgements

· · ·

The author would like to extend his sincere appreciation to Alex Craig, John Baird, Alexandra Wallace, Betty Moore, David Marr, Ian Taylor, Tom McNulty and those who just wish to remain anonymous (in case it effects their promotion chances).

Your contributions were appreciated.

I hope I did them justice.

A special thank you to everyone at Black & White Publishing.

Next in the Harry the Polis Series:
There's Been A Murder! Volume 8
The End

Contact Details
Website: www.harrythepolis.com
Email: harry@harrythepolis.com

Harry Morris aka 'Harry the Polis', is available for Stand-Up Humour, Storytelling, Guest Speaking, Script / Sketch Writing.

All enquiries to info@harrythepolis.com

Harry Morris is a member of the Society of Authors, a member of Equity and is also registered with the Scottish Book Trust for Live Literature events and workshops.